Portland Cooks

RECIPES FROM THE CITY'S
Best Restaurants & Bars

Portland Cooks

DANIELLE CENTONI

Figure 1
Vancouver / Berkeley

Cataloguing data is available from Library and Archives Canada
ISBN 978-1-927958-93-3 (hbk.)

Design by Natalie Olsen
Photography by Leela Cyd
Prop styling by Anne Parker
Photography assistance by Celeste Noche
(portraits on page 12, 68, 138)
Ceramics by Alexandria Cummings and Dino No

Editing by Michelle Meade
Copy editing by Lana Okerlund
Proofreading by Lucy Kenward
Index by Iva Cheung

Printed and bound in China by C&C Offset Printing Co., Ltd.
Distributed in the U.S. by Publishers Group West

Figure 1 Publishing Inc.
Vancouver BC Canada
figure1publishing.com

For the chefs, whose back-breaking, adrenaline-fueled, no-weekends-off work fills our plates with comfort and joy. Thank you for keeping us so well fed.

Contents

Introduction

NOBODY SAW IT COMING, the national preoccupation with Portland's food scene. Nobody expected our sleepy, midsize city to be mentioned in the same breath as New York and San Francisco. We were in our own little blissed-out bubble, oblivious to the fact that the rest of the world didn't have a small-batch coffee roaster on every corner, local craft beer on every tap, and pedigreed chefs cooking in food carts.

What was newsworthy elsewhere was simply the way of life. Of course the bartenders made their own bitters. Of course the chefs went foraging. Of course they made by hand or locally sourced everything, from the rooftop honey to the charcuterie. We never quite realized how spoiled we were until the articles arrived in a steady stream, month after month: the *New York Times*, *Travel + Leisure*, *Bon Appétit*, the *Wall Street Journal*, the *New York Times* again, and again. And then came the James Beard nominations, followed by wins, followed by tourists coming just to eat and drink.

Portland, it turns out, was on the cutting edge without ever trying to be, and now our city is synonymous with DIY scrappiness,

rule-breaking creativity, and a die-hard collaborative spirit. They're even recreating our restaurants in Tokyo — lock, stock, and barrel.

We get it now. We know how lucky we are. And if we forget, it only takes a trip out of town to remind us. It wasn't always like this, though, despite Portland's claim to fame as the hometown of James Beard himself. How did we get from ho-hum to "big in Japan?"

You could say it's our geography, a city encircled by family farms, world-class wineries, forageable forests, and a stone's throw from the bountiful sea. The ingredients at our fingertips are nothing short of inspiring.

You could say the relatively cheap rent, and even cheaper liquor licenses, makes it easier for entrepreneurial chefs and artisan producers to strike out on their own, free to follow their bliss without any corporate handcuffs.

Or you could say it's in our culture, a captive audience of curious and knowledgeable food lovers who know their Hood strawberries from their Seascapes, who welcome culinary risk taking, who don't stand for mediocrity. You can try anything here, but it better be good.

I say it's all of those things, but they would mean nothing without our deep pool of talent in front of the stoves and behind the bars. The uncompromising creativity of the chefs, bartenders, restaurateurs, and food producers driving our food scene is our richest resource. And that's what this book is all about.

These pages are a celebration of the pioneers, game changers, upstarts, and torch bearers who help put Portland on the culinary map. These are the talents at the beating heart of it all, and they're graciously sharing some of their greatest hits with us. Some recipes are an adventure, requiring a trip to the Asian market, while others are a snap to pull off on any given weeknight. But they're all fantastic and eminently doable (and we have an army of home-cook recipe testers to prove it).

Through their recipes, these chefs and bartenders offer a glimpse of what goes into your favorite dishes and drinks. And together, their stories paint a portrait of what makes life in Portland so delicious.

The Restaurants

The Recipes

Acadia Bistro

IN AN INDUSTRY marked by constant change, from itinerant staff to seasonal booms and busts, it's rare to find a chef who has the dedication to stay put—and continues to evolve in the process. Seamus Foran is one such rarity. A Portland native, he walked into charming Acadia Bistro as a pantry cook 10 years ago and quickly earned the mantle of sous chef. For eight years, he worked the stoves before taking the leap two years ago to add owner to his title.

Clearly Acadia is his heart and soul, and clearly he's doing a lot of things right, because this little Cajun spot in the middle of a sleepy Northeast Portland neighborhood brings in devotees from all across town, and beyond.

They come for the spot-on étouffée swimming with Louisiana blue crab and crawfish tails, or the belly-filling po' boys stuffed with house-made Andouille sausage, or the super-fresh Gulf shrimp, sautéed Cajun-style with plenty of butter and spice. And they keep coming back, week after week, year after year, with a dedication to this place that's matched only by the chef himself.

INGREDIENTS

6 cups heavy cream

6 eggs

6 egg yolks

2 cups granulated sugar

1 Tbsp pure vanilla extract

1 lb loaf stale French bread
(not baguette), cut into 1-inch
cubes (about 10 cups)

Warm caramel sauce, to serve

Acadia's Bread Pudding *Serves 10*

For this quintessential Cajun dessert, chef/owner Seamus Foran hews to tradition with a simple but decadent mix of vanilla-scented cream and a heap of eggs. It's fantastic drizzled with a little caramel sauce. And if you're not planning to use up the leftover egg whites in an omelet, freeze them until you get a craving for angel food cake or meringues.

METHOD Pour the cream into a large saucepan and bring to a simmer over medium-high heat.

Meanwhile, in a large bowl, whisk together the eggs, yolks, sugar, and vanilla. Gradually pour the hot cream into the bowl, whisking continuously to avoid curdling the eggs.

Preheat oven to 350°F. Butter a 9- × 13-inch pan and add the bread cubes. Pour the egg and cream mixture over the bread and press down to make sure all pieces are saturated. Allow to sit for 15 to 20 minutes, until the bread has fully absorbed the liquid.

Bake for 45 minutes. Reduce heat to 300°F and bake for another 15 minutes, or until set and golden brown and a knife inserted in the center comes out clean. Serve warm with caramel sauce.

INGREDIENTS

1 Tbsp plus 1 ½ tsp Creole
  seasoning (such as Seafood Magic
  or Cajun's Choice)

2 Tbsp freshly ground black pepper

2 cloves garlic, finely chopped

3 Tbsp Worcestershire sauce

1 Tbsp vegetable oil

1 lb jumbo Louisiana shrimp (u/15 count),
  peeled, heads and tails on

Salt

1 lemon wedge

½ cup dry white wine

½ cup shrimp or seafood stock

10 Tbsp (1 ¼ sticks) cold unsalted
  butter, cut into cubes

4 scallions, chopped, for garnish

French bread, to serve

New Orleans BBQ Shrimp *Serves 4*

Acadia's BBQ Shrimp is one of its most popular appetizers, a dish so beloved it can never leave the menu. But it's not actually barbecued at all. In New Orleans, "BBQ" refers to the buttery, Cajun-spiced sauce that coats this classic dish of sautéed shrimp. It's incredibly simple to make, but chef Seamus Foran explains that the success of this dish depends greatly on the quality of your shrimp; look for firm, wild-caught varieties from America's Gulf Coast. Be sure to serve this with plenty of crusty bread for mopping up the sauce.

METHOD In a small bowl, combine the Creole seasoning, pepper, garlic, and Worcestershire sauce. Mix until a loose paste is formed.

Heat the oil in a medium saucepan or skillet over medium-high heat until almost smoking. Add the shrimp and a pinch of salt and cook for 1 to 2 minutes, until the shrimp begin to color. Add the spice paste and toss to coat. Squeeze the lemon juice into the pan, then toss in the whole wedge. Sauté the shrimp for another 1 to 2 minutes, until cooked through. Transfer to a plate.

Add the wine and stock to the pan, stirring to scrape up the browned bits. Cook for 5 minutes, or until the stock is reduced by half. Reduce heat to medium-low and whisk in the cubed butter. Stir until melted and incorporated. (Do not boil or the butter might separate; moving the pan on and off the heat will help prevent your sauce from breaking.)

Return the shrimp to the pan and toss to coat in the sauce. Taste and adjust the seasoning, if desired. Transfer to a serving bowl or platter, sprinkle with scallions, and serve alongside warm French bread.

Andina

WITH ITS TONY Pearl District address, imposing brick façade, superlative cocktails, and elegant plating, it's easy to see why always-busy Andina is perennially at the top of Portland's power-lunch and date-night lists. But by the same token, it's easy to forget that the Peruvian hotspot is, at its heart, a humble mom-and-pop restaurant—a place that prizes heritage, hospitality, and family above any of the latest trends. Of course, all you have to do is dine there to be reminded, as Peru native Doris "Mama" Rodriguez de Platt works the room and tells the story of the family and the country's culinary history.

With it still going strong after 14 years, it's crazy to think that Andina began pretty much on a lark. Peter Platt, son of Doris and her

Oregonian husband, John, wanted to share his Peruvian culture with his home state through the platform of food. His parents and brothers, John Jr. and Victor, soon joined the adventure, and the rest is history.

Be forewarned, however, that any visit to Andina will surely inspire another… and another. It takes time to make your way through the extensive menu, with its pisco cocktails muddled with cucumber and elderflower tonic, *cebiches* of plump shellfish bathed in "tiger's milk," and bowls of duck confit with cilantro rice and piquant passion fruit sauce. It's a menu as varied as the Peruvian landscape, and you're going to want to try it all.

1 cup white quinoa

1 cup red quinoa

4 cups water, or chicken or vegetable broth

Salt

1 avocado, diced

½ cucumber, peeled and diced (about 1 cup, divided)

2 Roma tomatoes, seeded and diced (about 1 cup, divided)

1 Tbsp chopped fresh mint, plus extra for garnish

1 Tbsp chopped fresh cilantro

1 Tbsp chopped fresh Italian parsley

3 Tbsp extra-virgin olive oil

Juice of 3 limes (about ½ cup, divided)

11 botija or kalamata olives, pitted and cut into thin strips

3 Tbsp crumbled Cotija or feta

1 ear corn, cooked, kernels cut off (about ¾ cup)

1 yellow bell pepper, cut into matchsticks

½ red onion, cut into matchsticks

Quinoa Tabbouleh *Serves 4* *(main course) or 8 to 10 (side dish)*

This South American take on the classic Middle Eastern grain salad replaces the bulgur wheat with two kinds of quinoa and includes a handful of corn for a distinctly Peruvian touch. It travels well and is as gorgeous as it is flavorful, making it a great option for your next potluck.

METHOD Combine both types of quinoa in a fine-mesh strainer and rinse well under cold water. In a saucepan, combine the quinoa and water (or broth). Season with salt to taste. Bring to a boil over high heat, reduce the heat to low, cover, and simmer for 20 to 25 minutes, until water is absorbed and quinoa is tender. Spread the quinoa on a baking sheet to cool and fluff.

In a mixing bowl, combine the cooled quinoa, avocado, half of the cucumbers, half of the tomatoes, and the herbs. Mix well. Drizzle with the olive oil and half of the lime juice, and toss to coat. Season with salt to taste. Transfer to a serving bowl.

In another bowl, mix the remaining cucumbers and tomatoes with the olives, cheese, corn kernels, yellow peppers, and onions. Season with salt and the remaining lime juice. Spoon the mixture over the quinoa and garnish with mint leaves.

"TIGER'S MILK"
1 cup freshly squeezed lime juice
  (about 5 limes)
¼ cup chopped red onion
¼ cup whitefish trimmings
2 cloves garlic
1 stalk celery, roughly chopped
½ aji limo pepper or habanero
  pepper, seeded (see Note)

1 Tbsp chopped fresh ginger
Salt, to taste
¼ cup chopped cilantro stems
½ cup ice
CEBICHE
1 small red onion
1 sweet potato, peeled and
  sliced into ¾-inch-thick rounds
Salt

1 ear corn
1 ¼ lb boneless, skinless whitefish such
  as sea bass, red snapper, or grouper
½ aji limo pepper or habanero pepper
  (see Note)
¼ cup chopped fresh cilantro
1 cup "tiger's milk" (see here) or ½ cup
  freshly squeezed lime juice
4 leaves butter lettuce

Cebiche "Cinco Elementos"
Serves 4

Andina is known for its selection of sparkling fresh *cebiches*, including a version with green mango and prawns, but this one is the most popular and a true classic. The "tiger's milk," or *leche de tigre,* is simply the cream-colored juices that form when the fish, lime juice, and onion are mixed together. At the restaurant, they make a special batch of spiced-up tiger's milk to ensure that guests ordering this dish have plenty of flavorful liquid to scoop up with their spoons. If you like, you can skip that step and simply add ½ cup fresh lime juice directly to the *cebiche* ingredients, and they'll make their own tiger's milk. This dish is served with sweet potato and fresh corn to help tame its tart, spicy flavors.

Note: Aji limo peppers are little yellow peppers commonly used in Peruvian cuisine. They have a similar flavor and spice level to habanero peppers, which make a good substitute. Be sure to wash your hands thoroughly after handling, and avoid touching your eyes and nose.

"TIGER'S MILK" In a blender, place all ingredients except cilantro and ice and blend for 1 minute. Add cilantro and ice and pulse three times in 5-second intervals to blend. Strain and reserve 1 cup tiger's milk. (Refrigerate or freeze the rest for another use.)

CEBICHE Slice the onion in half top to bottom, remove the core at the root end, and slice into thin matchsticks. Soak in a bowl of ice water for 30 minutes.

Set a pot of water over high heat. Add the sweet potatoes, cover, and bring to a boil. Salt generously and cook for 6 minutes, or until easily pierced with a knife. Remove with a slotted spoon and allow to cool. Add the corn to the boiling water and cook for 2 minutes. Remove, and when cool enough to handle, slice into ¾-inch-thick rounds.

Cut the fish into ½-inch cubes. Add to the bowl with the onion, swish briefly, then strain out the fish and onion. Transfer them to a large bowl.

Remove the ribs and seeds from the pepper, rinse under cold water, and thinly slice. Add the sliced pepper and chopped cilantro to the bowl with the fish and onions. Stir in tiger's milk (or ½ cup fresh lime juice). Taste and season with more salt if necessary. Allow to sit for 10 minutes.

Arrange a butter lettuce leaf on one side of four shallow bowls and top with sweet potato and corn. Divide the *cebiche* among the bowls. Eat the *cebiche,* sweet potato, and lettuce with a spoon to capture all the liquid, and eat the corn with your fingers.

JOSE CHESA

Ataula
Chesa

WHEN A MICHELIN-STARRED chef turns his attention to tapas, good things happen. Humble fried potatoes become feats of culinary genius requiring trips through the sous vide machine. Simple slices of chorizo turn into cheese- and quince-stuffed lollipops that elevate food-on-a-stick to high art. It's thrilling and exciting and exactly the kind of cooking you'd expect to find in some high-profile hotspot in Manhattan, not a quiet little side street in Portland. And therein lies the charm. Ataula is a neighborhood spot, as fun, friendly, and unpretentious as they come. But it offers an exacting level of service and cuisine born from the high temples of haute where chef-owners Jose Chesa and his wife, Cristina Báez, honed their craft.

Luckily for Portland, the two decided to put down roots in our neck of the woods, elevating our restaurant scene in the process. In early 2016, the duo expanded their reach, opening paella-focused Chesa, complete with a daytime churro shop called 180 next door. Named in honor of Jose's father, Chesa has a bit more gravitas than their original spot, and the dishes are prepared with the same dedication. Each paella is layered with rich flavor and cooked à *la minute* in a charcoal-fired Josper oven, giving it that requisite kiss of smoke.

Pictured: Salt Cod Croquetas

Salt Cod Croquetas

Makes about 4 dozen

Bite into these crispy fritters and you'll find a rich center of creamy *bacalao,* or salt cod, enriched with luscious cream sauce. There's a reason why they're one of the most popular items on Ataula's menu.

Note: Salt cod is dried, heavily salted cod fish. You can find it at specialty stores or online gourmet retailers. Look for packages that contain pieces from the center of the fish rather than from the tail, which can be stringy.

CROQUETAS Rinse the cod well under cold running water. Set the cod in a large bowl and cover with several inches of cold water. Refrigerate for 24 hours, changing the water at least twice. Taste the cod. It should be salty enough that no additional salt is needed to make the croquetas. If it's still too salty, you can change the water and let it soak longer. Remove the cod from the water and roughly chop.

Heat the oil in a medium pot set over medium heat. Add the onion and sauté until tender, about 5 minutes. Add the garlic and sauté for another minute. Transfer to a food processor and add the salt cod and parsley. Pulse to create a chunky paste.

CROQUETAS

1 lb boneless, skinless salt cod
   fillets (see Note)
1 Tbsp extra-virgin olive oil
½ large onion, chopped
3 cloves garlic, chopped
¼ cup chopped fresh Italian
   parsley

BÉCHAMEL

¾ cup (1 ½ sticks) unsalted butter
1 cup all-purpose flour
2 cups whole milk
Salt and freshly ground black pepper

ASSEMBLY

½ cup all-purpose flour
2 eggs, well beaten
2 to 3 cups panko
Canola oil, for frying
Freshly ground black pepper
1 cup Aioli (page 21), for serving
Microgreens and edible flowers,
   for garnish (optional)

BÉCHAMEL Melt the butter in a large saucepan over medium heat. Stir in the flour and cook for 1 to 2 minutes. Whisk in the milk, a little at a time, letting the roux absorb the liquid before adding more. Allow to simmer gently over medium heat for 10 minutes, until thick enough to coat the back of a spoon.

Add the salt cod mixture to the béchamel and stir continuously with a wooden spoon until completely blended, about 10 minutes. (Stirring is the key to a good croqueta!) Taste and season with salt and pepper, if needed. Set aside to cool, then cover and refrigerate overnight. (If you want to make the croquetas the same day, you can spread the mixture onto a rimmed baking sheet so it will cool faster.)

ASSEMBLY Use a small ice cream scoop to portion out heaping tablespoon-size balls of the cold croqueta mixture. Roll between your hands to form a smooth ball and place on a rimmed baking sheet.

Place the flour, beaten eggs, and panko in three separate bowls. Set a large cooling rack nearby. Roll each croqueta in flour, shaking off the excess. Coat each in the egg, then roll in the panko until fully coated. Set on the cooling rack and repeat with the remaining croquetas. (To keep your fingers from getting gummed up, use one hand for dipping in the egg and the other hand for rolling in panko.) Allow to air dry on the rack for 15 to 20 minutes to help the crumbs adhere and result in a crispier croqueta. (Croquetas can be made up to a day ahead and refrigerated.)

In a large saucepan set over medium heat, or in a deep fryer, heat at least 4 inches of oil to 350°F (this can take 10 to 20 minutes). Line a baking sheet with paper towels and set aside. Working in batches, fry the croquetas for 5 minutes, turning frequently, until golden brown. Remove with a slotted spoon and place on paper towels to drain. Sprinkle with black pepper and serve warm garnished with aioli and microgreens and edible flowers, if using.

FISH STOCK

3 lb whitefish bones and heads
  (see Note)

1 Tbsp kosher salt, plus more to taste

1 Tbsp extra-virgin olive oil

2 shallots, roughly chopped

1 carrot, chopped

2 stalks celery, chopped

1 cup chopped shiitake mushrooms

3 whole black peppercorns

5 cloves garlic, chopped

½ cup white wine

6 cups water

½ bunch fresh thyme

Arroz Negro

Serves 6

This bold paella-style rice dish gets its jet-black color from squid ink. A dollop of pale aioli on top makes the presentation even more dramatic. Jose and Cristina say it's delicious with a simple green salad and a glass of cold beer, dry sherry, or *txakolí,* a sparkling dry white wine from the Basque region.

Notes: Call your fishmonger to reserve bones, heads, and tails from whitefish such as halibut, cod, snapper, or sole. Avoid bones from oily fish such as salmon, which are too strongly flavored. | Bomba rice is a short-grain rice traditionally used for paella. You can find it, usually in cloth bags, at well-stocked grocery stores or online retailers. Squid ink is a little harder to find. Look for it at gourmet markets and online retailers. It is often either sealed in small, shelf-stable packets or refrigerated or frozen in small jars.

FISH STOCK Makes 4 cups. This makes more than you'll need for the paella, but you can freeze it for up to three months before it begins to lose flavor.

Place fish bones and heads in a large bowl (if necessary, cut to fit). Cover with cold water and stir in the salt. Allow to sit for 1 hour to purge the blood. Rinse well.

Meanwhile, heat the olive oil in a stockpot over medium heat. Sauté the shallots, carrot, celery, mushrooms, and peppercorns for 5 minutes, until the shallots are translucent. Add the garlic and sauté for another 3 minutes.

Add the fish bones and heads. Pour in the wine, stirring to scrape up any browned bits. Add the water and thyme and season lightly with salt. Bring to a simmer over medium-high heat and cook, uncovered, for 20 to 30 minutes. Strain and use immediately or refrigerate for up to 48 hours.

PAELLA

2 Tbsp extra-virgin olive oil (divided)
1 onion, diced
3 cloves garlic, finely chopped
½ red bell pepper, diced
½ green bell pepper, diced
2 Roma tomatoes, seeded and diced
2 tsp smoked paprika (pimentón)
Salt and freshly ground black pepper
2 ½ to 3 cups fish stock (see here, or
   use store-bought)
½ lb cleaned squid, cut into ¼-inch
   strips, tentacles left whole or halved
1 ¼ cups bomba rice (see Note)
2 Tbsp squid ink (see Note)

AIOLI

1 egg
2 cloves garlic, crushed
Salt
1 cup grapeseed oil or other
   neutral vegetable oil

ASSEMBLY

1 Tbsp extra-virgin olive oil
½ lb cuttlefish, cut into ¼-inch strips,
   or jumbo shrimp (u/15 count), peeled
   and deveined
Salt and freshly ground black pepper
¼ cup finely chopped fresh Italian
   parsley
5 piquillo peppers in oil, thinly sliced
Lemon wedges, for serving

PAELLA Preheat oven to 450°F. Heat 1 tablespoon of the olive oil in a 12-inch paella pan or large frying pan set over medium heat. Add the onion and sauté for 7 minutes, or until translucent. Add the garlic and sauté for another minute. Add both peppers and cook until softened. Add the tomatoes, smoked paprika, salt, and pepper and cook until all liquid has been released. Set pan aside.

Bring the stock to a simmer in a small saucepan. Set a medium sauté pan over medium-high heat. Add another tablespoon of the oil and the squid. Season with salt and pepper to taste and sauté until tender, about 1 to 2 minutes. Add the squid and the rice to the tomato mixture in the large paella pan, set over medium heat, and cook, stirring, for 2 to 3 minutes, until the edges of the rice are translucent but the center is still white.

Stir 2 ½ cups of the hot broth into the pan, then add the squid ink. Season with salt and pepper to taste. Increase heat to medium-high, bring liquid to a boil, then transfer the pan to the oven. Cook, uncovered, for 15 to

20 minutes, until the liquid is absorbed but the rice is not quite done. Add the remaining ½ cup stock if the rice seems too dry and needs to cook longer.

Set the paella pan over high heat and cook for 3 minutes to create a *socarrat* (crispy bottom crust). Remove from heat, cover lightly with foil, and let it rest for 10 minutes while you make the aioli.

AIOLI Combine the egg, crushed garlic, and a pinch of salt in a food processor or blender. With the machine running, very slowly add the oil in a thin, steady stream until incorporated and mixture is emulsified.

ASSEMBLY Heat oil in the medium sauté pan over medium-high heat. Season the cuttlefish (or shrimp) with salt and pepper to taste. Sauté until tender, about 1 to 2 minutes. Remove from heat and stir in the parsley. Arrange the cuttlefish (or shrimp) and the piquillo peppers on top of the paella. Add a dollop of aioli in the center. Serve the paella with lemon wedges and pass the remaining aioli at the table.

Milk Glass Mrkt

SARAH PLINER

Aviary

IF YOU'RE A FIRST-TIMER at Aviary, you might find the menu puzzling. It's more ambitious and cerebral than you'd expect from the laid-back space, and you might be surprised to see rice bowls topped with crispy pig's ears alongside salads of fried chicken skin, watermelon, and baba ghanoush. What is going on here? you might ask yourself. What did I just walk into? Just take a deep breath and then take the plunge, because although you're in the wilds of chef-owner Sarah Pliner's culinary genius, you're also in her very capable hands.

The fact that Pliner went to Portland's unabashedly creative and fiercely intellectual Reed College speaks volumes. Add to that her years working in the Michelin-starred kitchens of Aquavit and Aldea in New York and, well, all of a sudden Aviary makes perfect sense. At her seven-year-old restaurant in the Alberta Arts District, Pliner uses global flavors, particularly those from Asian cuisines, like an artist with a giant box of paints. She adheres not to tradition, but to flavor, creating an eclectic, modern menu that defies easy description, but does so deliciously.

2 (12 oz) packages silken soft tofu,
  cut in half widthwise

¼ cup low-sodium soy sauce

2 Tbsp Chinkiang vinegar (Chinese
  black vinegar)

2 tsp granulated sugar (divided)

3 Tbsp fermented hot bean paste
  (such as O'Long brand)

3 Tbsp extra-virgin olive oil (divided)

3 scallions, thinly sliced

½ cup diced cantaloupe

2 Tbsp chopped fresh cilantro leaves

2 Tbsp thinly sliced tiato leaves
  (see Note)

2 tsp grated fresh ginger

Salt

¼ cup toasted sesame seeds, crushed

¼ cup chopped roasted peanuts

Zest of 1 lime

Chilled Tofu with Scallions, Cantaloupe, and Hot Bean Paste *Serves 4*

The interplay of cool and silky tofu with a spicy, flavor-packed sauce makes this dish downright addictive. Although you might not have Chinese black vinegar and hot bean paste on hand, they're readily available at Asian markets and worth the pantry space—the robust vinegar is excellent in braised greens, and the bean paste will transform your stir-fries.

Note: Tiato is an Asian herb that looks like shiso but is smaller, with a purple hue under the leaves, and has a similar yet stronger flavor. You can usually find it at Asian markets, particularly those that specialize in Vietnamese ingredients. If you can't find it, substitute shiso leaves.

METHOD Place the tofu in the bottom of four shallow bowls.

In a small bowl, mix together the soy sauce, black vinegar, and 1 teaspoon sugar. Pour the mixture over the tofu. In the same bowl, mix together the bean paste, 1 tablespoon olive oil, and the remaining 1 teaspoon sugar. Use a spoon to spread the paste on top of each tofu.

In a medium bowl, mix together the scallions, cantaloupe, cilantro, *tiato*, ginger, and the remaining 2 tablespoons olive oil. Season with salt to taste. Mound on top of each tofu. Garnish each with sesame seeds, peanuts, and lime zest.

DASHI

4 cups cold water

3-inch piece dry kombu

1-inch piece fresh ginger,
    peeled and thinly sliced

2 Tbsp soy sauce

2 Tbsp mirin

½ cup bonito flakes

TRUFFLE VINAIGRETTE

1 Tbsp extra-virgin olive oil

½ yellow onion, thinly sliced

½ tsp salt

1 oz fresh truffles or canned black
    truffles, thinly sliced (see Note)

1 Tbsp sherry vinegar

1 tsp Dijon mustard

⅓ cup cold water

½ cup grapeseed oil or neutral
    vegetable oil

A few drops of black truffle oil

Dungeness Crab
Chawanmushi *Serves 4*

Chawanmushi, or steamed Japanese egg custards, are usually quite simple in flavor, but not at Aviary, where they're topped with a truffle salad, bone marrow, and sea urchin roe. That might seem daunting to recreate, but the components are actually easy to make and can be prepared in advance. However, feel free to simplify the toppings as you see fit. The vinaigrette makes about 2 cups, which is more than you need, but it keeps well and is delicious on a variety of salads.

Notes: Fresh truffles are seasonal, and expensive, making canned truffles an economical year-round alternative. The only trouble is that the products vary quite a lot in intensity. When adding truffles to the vinaigrette, start with a little and taste as you go until it's to your liking. | *Wood ear mushrooms are dark-colored and commonly used in Chinese dishes like hot and sour soup, where they are prized for their chewy texture and mild flavor. Look for packages of the dried mushrooms (often labeled "fungus" or "auricula-judae") at Asian markets.* | *Ask your butcher for pipe bones (long cylindrical marrow bones) that are open on both sides, because they are the easiest to pop marrow out of. To prepare the marrow, preheat*

oven to 400°F. Place the marrow bones on a baking sheet and roast for 3 to 4 minutes. When cool enough to handle, scrape around the inside of the bone, then use your thumb, or a blunt tool, to push the marrow out. Put the marrow in cold water with just a splash of white vinegar for at least 4 hours to purge the blood. | *You can buy sea urchin roe, or uni, at well-stocked fish markets, online retailers, or some Asian markets.*

DASHI In a medium saucepan, combine the water, kombu, ginger, soy sauce, and mirin. Bring to a boil, reduce heat to low, and very slowly simmer for 1 hour. Add the bonito flakes and remove from heat. Allow to sit for 10 minutes. Strain through a fine-mesh strainer and refrigerate until cold. You should have 1 ½ cups. (Dashi can be made several days ahead.)

TRUFFLE VINAIGRETTE Heat the olive oil in a small saucepan over medium heat. Add the onion and salt and gently cook until soft and translucent, about 5 minutes. Add the truffles and vinegar and cook another 5 minutes.

CHAWANMUSHI

6 oz crabmeat, picked through
    for shells

3 eggs

SALAD

⅓ cup dried wood ear mushrooms
    (see Note)

15 sugar snap peas, blanched and
    cut into matchsticks

½ Asian pear, peeled and diced

1 thick slice brioche or brioche roll,
    cut into ½-inch cubes and toasted
    in the oven

5 chives, thinly sliced

ASSEMBLY

Roasted marrow from 2 (2-inch)
    marrow bones (see Note)

4 large or 8 small pieces uni
    (optional, see Note)

In a blender, combine the onion mixture, mustard, and water and purée until smooth. With the blender on low speed, gradually add the grapeseed oil and truffle oil. If the mixture gets too thick or breaks, thin out with a little cold water and blend. (Vinaigrette can be made several days ahead and refrigerated.)

CHAWANMUSHI Preheat oven to 300°F. Bring a pot or kettle of water to a boil.

Divide the crabmeat among four small bowls or ramekins. Place the bowls in a roasting pan. Whisk together the eggs and 1 ½ cups dashi in a medium bowl. Divide the egg mixture among the bowls, covering the crab. Pour hot water into the roasting pan to come halfway up the side of the bowls. Cover the pan with foil and bake for 30 to 60 minutes, or until the custard has set. (The timing depends on how big your roasting pan is and how hot the water is. Begin checking close to 30 minutes. If they're almost fully set, you know they're almost done. If they're still quite liquidy, you know you have a ways to go.) Remove the *chawanmushis* from the roasting pan.

SALAD Place the mushrooms in a medium bowl, cover with warm water, and set aside for 10 minutes to rehydrate. Drain. If there is a tough nub at the bottom, cut it off and discard. Thinly slice the mushrooms and set aside.

In a small bowl, toss the mushrooms, snap peas, pears, brioche, and chives with just enough truffle vinaigrette to coat (about 2 tablespoons).

ASSEMBLY Using a knife dipped in hot water, slice the bone marrow into 16 slices. Fan 4 slices on top of each custard, and either lightly brown with a torch or pop it briefly under the broiler in the oven, to melt just a little.

Top each custard with some of the salad. If using uni, place one or two pieces in the center of each. Serve warm.

CANA FLUG & DUSTIN CLARK

Besaw's

HUMBLE BESAW'S, with its hex tile entry and creaky wood floors, stood on the corner of Northwest 23rd Avenue for more than 100 years, a living reminder of the neighborhood's working-class roots, before the "Trendy-Third" boutiques moved in. And for more than 100 years, generations of loyal locals packed into this tiny but beloved corner of Slabtown to tuck into a belly-warming brunch of eggs Benedict with silky hollandaise, fuel up with a juicy burger and a pint at lunch, or celebrate a night out with a gorgeous rib-eye steak for dinner.

But this Portland institution had been bursting at the seams for far too long, and in 2016 it moved into a brand-new building just a few blocks away. What it lost in vintage cred it more than gained in amenities like a properly sized commercial kitchen and ample elbow room, resulting in a slightly more ambitious menu from executive chef Dustin Clark and weekend brunch lines that aren't quite so long. And though the building is all shiny new construction, owner Cana Flug infused old-school charm into every nook and cranny. The new Besaw's looks like it's been there forever, and Flug and her team have proven that it wasn't the building that made it so special, it was the synergy between the devoted staff and loyal community—and a lineup of perfectly executed comfort food that brings you back for more.

Pictured: Eggs Benedict with Roasted Garlic-Rosemary Potatoes

ROASTED POTATOES

8 cloves garlic, peeled

½ cup extra-virgin olive oil

1 lb Yukon Gold potatoes, cut into
    ¾-inch cubes

1 Tbsp chopped fresh rosemary

Salt and freshly ground black pepper

Eggs Benedict with Roasted Garlic-Rosemary Potatoes *Serves 4*

Besaw's is known for classic brunch dishes like this, made with strict attention to detail. Although you can make hollandaise with simply melted butter, the restaurant uses clarified butter because it results in the smoothest, silkiest texture. Clarifying butter isn't hard, but you can skip this step and simply melt it, or buy store-bought clarified butter (or ghee) at well-stocked supermarkets.

ROASTED POTATOES Preheat oven to 425°F. Combine the garlic and olive oil in a small saucepan set over medium-low heat and poach the garlic for 10 minutes, until tender.

Meanwhile, bring a large pot of salted water to a boil and add the diced potatoes. Cook for 10 to 12 minutes, until just tender. Drain.

Remove the garlic with a slotted spoon, transfer to a cutting board, and finely chop. On a baking sheet, toss the cooked potatoes with the garlic oil, rosemary, and salt and pepper to taste. Roast for 35 to 40 minutes, or until golden brown. Add the garlic and toss until evenly distributed.

REDUCTION Combine all reduction ingredients in a small saucepan over medium heat and simmer for several minutes, until reduced by three-quarters. Strain out the solids and discard. Cool the liquid to room temperature. (Reduction can be made several days ahead.)

HOLLANDAISE Melt the butter in a saucepan set over medium heat. Allow to simmer, spooning off the white froth as it rises to the surface, until there's no more froth and the milk solids accumulate on the bottom and sides of the pan. Remove from heat and let the solids settle for a few minutes. Pour off the clear, golden butter into a measuring cup, leaving the solids behind (you can also use a fine-mesh or cheesecloth-lined strainer). You should have 1 cup.

Bring a double boiler or saucepan with water to a gentle simmer. In a stainless steel bowl or the top of the double boiler (off the heat), whisk the yolks and water

REDUCTION

2 Tbsp champagne vinegar or
  quality white wine vinegar
2 Tbsp white wine
1 Tbsp finely chopped shallots
10 whole black peppercorns
1 bay leaf, crumbled

HOLLANDAISE

1 ¼ cups (2 ½ sticks) unsalted butter
3 egg yolks
1 Tbsp water
1 Tbsp freshly squeezed lemon juice
Pinch of cayenne
Salt

ASSEMBLY

2 Tbsp distilled white vinegar
8 large eggs
8 slices Canadian bacon
4 English muffins
¼ cup (½ stick) unsalted butter
Fresh Italian parsley or other
  soft herbs, chopped (optional)

together for 30 seconds, until frothy. Set over the barely simmering water (the water should not touch the bowl) and continue whisking for 4 minutes, until the mixture is thickened and light in color. (The whisk should leave lines through the mixture that reveal the bottom of the pan. If necessary, remove the bowl from heat periodically to keep the eggs from getting too hot and scrambling. If the mixture scrambles, you must start over.)

Remove bowl from heat and whisk for a few seconds to cool the mixture a bit. Gradually add the 1 cup of butter in a thin, steady stream, whisking constantly, until emulsified (go slow or the sauce might break). Whisk in the reduction, lemon juice, and cayenne. Season with salt to taste. Cover the sauce and keep in a warm place until serving, or set over the saucepan of still-hot (but not simmering) water.

ASSEMBLY Bring a large skillet of water to a steady simmer over medium-high heat and add the vinegar. Crack an egg into a ramekin or cup. Slowly tip the egg into the water, whites first. Repeat with the remaining eggs. When whites begin to set, use a rubber spatula to gently move them around to prevent them from sticking. Cook at a slow simmer for 3 to 4 minutes, until the whites are completely set and yolks are soft but no longer raw. (Eggs can be poached ahead. Keep warm in a bowl of warm water until serving. Or make a day ahead, refrigerate, and when ready to serve, rewarm cold eggs in a saucepan of gently simmering water.)

Sear Canadian bacon in a sauté pan set over medium-high heat. Toast the English muffins and spread with butter. Set two muffin halves on each plate and top each with a slice of Canadian bacon and a poached egg. Spoon hollandaise on top and sprinkle with herbs. Serve with the roasted potatoes.

SHALLOT BUTTER

½ cup red wine

2 large shallots, sliced

1 ½ tsp balsamic vinegar

½ cup (1 stick) unsalted
  butter, softened

FENNEL-DELICATA GRATIN

Butter, for greasing

1 bulb fennel, thinly sliced

1 delicata squash, cut in half lengthwise,
  seeds removed, and thinly sliced

1 onion, sliced

1 ½ cups shredded aged cheddar (divided)

½ cup heavy cream

1 Tbsp finely chopped fresh sage

1 Tbsp freshly squeezed lemon juice

Salt and freshly ground black pepper

ASSEMBLY

4 bone-in rib-eye steaks
  (about 1 ½ inches thick)

Salt and freshly ground black pepper

4 ½ cups watercress

3 Tbsp extra-virgin olive oil

2 Tbsp freshly squeezed lemon juice

Grilled Rib-Eye Steaks with Shallot Butter and Fennel-Delicata Squash Gratin *Serves 4*

Shallots braised in red wine and balsamic, then blended into creamy butter, form a deliciously luxe topping for grilled rib-eye steaks. The compound butter keeps well and is delicious with pork and chicken too.

SHALLOT BUTTER Combine wine, shallots, and vinegar in a saucepan over medium heat. Cook for about 10 minutes, until the shallots are tender and liquid has reduced. Set aside to cool.

In a food processor, combine the butter and shallot mixture and process until well combined. Scrape the butter out onto a sheet of plastic wrap. Mold into a log and wrap tightly in the plastic. Roll the wrapped butter back and forth on the counter to create a smooth, round log. Refrigerate until ready to use. (For longer storage, wrap the butter log in a piece of foil, label, and freeze.)

FENNEL-DELICATA GRATIN Preheat oven to 350°F. Butter a 9- × 13-inch baking dish. Combine the fennel, squash (the skin is edible, so there's no need to peel it), onion

and half the cheese in the dish. Mix together the cream, sage, lemon juice, and salt and pepper to taste. Pour over the vegetables. Sprinkle the remaining cheese on top. Cover with foil and bake for 45 minutes. Remove foil and bake for another 10 minutes, or until the cheese is golden brown. Remove from the oven and let rest for 10 minutes before serving.

ASSEMBLY Allow the steaks to sit at room temperature for 1 hour before cooking. Preheat grill to hot. If using a gas grill, leave one side unlit; if using a charcoal grill, keep the coals to one side. Pat steaks dry and season generously on both sides with salt and pepper. Grill the steaks on the hot side of the grill for 3 minutes, until seared. Turn and sear the other side for another 3 minutes. Transfer to the cool side of the grill, cover, and cook for 8 minutes, until medium-rare. Transfer to serving plates and let the meat rest for 7 minutes.

In a medium bowl, toss the watercress with olive oil and lemon juice. Divide the watercress and the gratin among the plates. Top the steaks with shallot butter and serve.

Besaw's

JESSE CARD & RICKY BELLA

Bit House Saloon

IT'S NOT EASY for a new place to look like it's been there forever, but when it does, you can't help but feel right at home. Such is the case with Bit House Saloon, "coined in 2015," as the logo states, but looking for all the world like it started life when the building's last stone was laid in the 1890s. With impossibly tall ceilings, exposed brick, and weathered wood trim, plus just enough random ephemera to feel authentic instead of overdesigned, Bit House bridges the gap between neighborhood hangout and destination bar perfectly.

It's a vibe carried through from the service all the way to the menu. Bar manager Jesse Card has assembled a team of crack bartenders who spent time in some of the most rigorous cocktail dens in the city. Together they bring deep expertise coupled with infectious playfulness. The result is serious cocktails that are

seriously fun. Single-barrel spirits and cocktails like margaritas flow from taps, which you can then opt to spike with a flavor of your choice (jalapeño or cucumber, perhaps?). Frozen boozy slushies appear alongside adult Otter Pops. Even boilermakers get ample consideration, with a dozen options like the Dead Elvis, which pairs bacon- and banana-infused rum with peanut butter stout. Chef Ricky Bella's menu takes the same approach. Familiar pub fare is crafted with refinement, and even guilty pleasures like fried bologna sandwiches get the housemade treatment. It's no surprise that Bit House was an instant hit from the moment it opened. At only two years old, it's already so beloved we can't even remember what life was like without it.

5 to 7 medium-size beets, tops
   and root ends trimmed

1 cup white wine

1 navel orange, sliced

1 bunch fresh oregano sprigs,
   plus 1 tsp chopped

1 bunch scallions, sliced diagonally

½ serrano pepper, thinly sliced
   (ribs and seeds removed if desired)

Juice of 1 lime

Salt and freshly ground black pepper

2 firm but ripe avocados

Extra-virgin olive oil, to brush

1 cup smoked or toasted pecans,
   roughly chopped (see Note)

1 Tbsp chopped fresh cilantro

Sea salt, for garnish

Roasted Beet Salad with Charred Avocado and Smoked Pecans *Serves 4 to 6*

Roasting the beets in a citrusy bath infuses them with flavor as they cook and makes them easy to peel. They get turned into a spicy salad that pairs deliciously with creamy charred avocado and smoked pecans, which give this vegan salad even more fresh-off-the-grill flavor (although toasted pecans will work too). Chef Ricky Bella says the dish was born from the idea of making beet salsa and just grew from there. Feel free to use a mix of red and gold beets, although you'll want to prepare them separately to preserve their color.

Note: Toast pecans in an even layer on a baking sheet in a 350°F oven for about 10 minutes, or until nutty and beginning to darken. To smoke pecans, soak in water for 10 minutes, then arrange in a grilling pan or foil pan with holes poked through the bottom. Smoke in a preheated smoker at 225°F for 20 to 30 minutes. Allow to cool until firm. To smoke the nuts in a charcoal grill, build a two-zone fire: pile 4 quarts of unlit charcoal on one side and top with 1 cup soaked wood chips. Top this with lit coals and another cup of soaked wood chips. Cover grill. When internal temperature reaches 225°F, place nuts on the grate opposite the fire. Smoke for 20 to 30 minutes. Allow to cool until firm.

METHOD Preheat oven to 350°F. Combine the beets, wine, orange slices, and oregano sprigs in a Dutch oven (just large enough to fit the beets). Add just enough water to cover the ingredients. Cover and roast for 40 to 50 minutes, or until fork-tender. Remove the beets and discard the remaining ingredients. When the beets are cool enough to handle, peel and dice. Allow to cool completely.

In a large bowl, combine the beets, scallions, serrano, lime juice, and remaining 1 teaspoon chopped oregano. Season with salt and pepper to taste.

Preheat grill to high heat. Cut the avocados in half and remove the pits. Brush the cut sides with olive oil and sprinkle with salt and pepper. Grill the avocados, cut side down, for 3 minutes, until charred and warm all the way through. Remove the skins and thinly slice.

Divide the avocados among the plates. Spoon the beet mixture over the avocados and garnish with smoked pecans, cilantro, and a sprinkle of sea salt.

MINT SYRUP
Makes 2 cups

2 cups granulated sugar

1 cup water

6 to 8 sprigs fresh mint, tied into
  a bundle with kitchen twine

Ice

COCKTAIL

2 oz 7 Sirens white rum

¾ oz freshly squeezed lemon juice

½ oz mint syrup (see here)

Dash of jasmine water, such as
  Fee Brothers

Pinch of beet powder (sold at
  natural food stores), plus more
  for garnish (optional)

Ice

3 oz soda water

Fresh mint sprig, for garnish

Lemon twist, for garnish

Sliced roasted beets, for garnish
  (optional)

K23 Cocktail

Serves 1

With cool mint, earthy beet powder, and a dash of jasmine water, Bit House Saloon's spritzy and vibrantly hued K23 Cocktail is not like anything you've ever had, but it totally works. Owner Jesse Card says it's named "for the elusive scent from Tom Robbins' novel *Jitterbug Perfume*. It's a conundrum of flavors all built on the heartiest of roots: the beet."

MINT SYRUP Combine the sugar and water in a medium saucepan set over medium-high heat. Bring to a simmer and cook for about 3 minutes, or until the sugar is completely dissolved and syrupy. Allow to cool.

Bring a small saucepan of water to a boil and set a bowl of ice water near the stove. Plunge the mint into the boiling water for 15 seconds. Remove with tongs or a slotted spoon and immediately submerge in a bowl of ice water for 1 minute, or until completely cool. Pat dry on a clean kitchen towel.

Remove the leaves from the mint stems. Add the leaves and simple syrup to a blender and blend for 1 minute. Strain the syrup through a fine-mesh strainer set over a bowl. Pour into an airtight container and refrigerate for up to 2 weeks.

COCKTAIL Combine rum, lemon juice, ½ oz mint syrup, jasmine water, beet powder, and ice in a cocktail shaker. Shake vigorously for 15 seconds. Double-strain over a short tumbler filled with crushed ice. Top with soda and garnish with a mint sprig, lemon twist, and beet powder or sliced roasted beets.

GABE ROSEN

Biwa Izakaya
Noraneko

PORTLAND HAS A serious Japanese food fetish, and in large part we have Gabe Rosen and Kina Voelz to thank for it. When the duo opened Biwa back in 2007, much of the city didn't know its *yakimono* from its *onigiri*, but their basement ode to Japan's drinking dens changed all that. Rosen translated his years eating and drinking his way through Japan into one of Portland's most beloved restaurants. In the process, he gave us an education in the ways of the *izakaya*, food-focused bars where umami, salt, and fat are the order of the day, intended to be washed down with ample booze, be it beer, sake, shochu, or cocktails.

Ten years later and the duo is still surprising us. In 2015, they opened their lunch-to-late-night ramen shop Noraneko, teaching us an appreciation for delicate, complex broths and bouncy noodles. And in 2016 they expanded once more, tightening up the original concept and turning it into the more sophisticated and intimate Biwa Izakaya just a few doors down. There, Japanophile chefs create sparkling sashimi plates, flavor-packed *otsumami* (Japanese snacks), and traditional dishes like *oden*, Japan's favorite winter stew. Meanwhile, the original space has been transformed into Parasol Bar, with an even more playful vibe and laid-back noodle dishes. All three places share a signature Portland-meets-Tokyo vibe and adhere to tradition without being slaves to it. It's a recipe for success that still keeps us lining up after all these years.

INGREDIENTS

1 lb skin-on chicken thighs, deboned

2 cups water

½ cup sake

½ cup kosher salt

½ cup soy sauce

1 Tbsp grated fresh ginger

4 scallions, sliced

1 ½ cups potato starch

½ cup cornstarch

Canola oil, for frying

Lemon wedges, to serve

Karaage

Serves 4

The Biwa/Noraneko team is very proud of its *karaage* (Japanese fried chicken), and with good reason. They traveled all over Japan eating every version they could get their hands on in order to develop this stellar recipe. It's fried in rice bran oil as well as chicken fat for extra deliciousness.

METHOD Cut the chicken thighs into 1- to 2-inch pieces. In a mixing bowl, combine the water, sake, salt, soy sauce, and ginger. Stir to dissolve the salt. Add the chicken, toss to coat, and allow to brine for 1 hour. Drain the chicken and mix with the scallions.

In a large mixing bowl, combine the potato starch and cornstarch. Add the chicken and toss until evenly and thoroughly coated.

In a large saucepan set over medium heat, or a deep fryer, heat at least 3 inches of oil to 360°F (this can take 10 to 20 minutes). Set a cooling rack on a baking sheet and place near the stove. Working in batches of about five pieces, deep-fry the chicken for 3 to 5 minutes, until golden and the internal temperature is 165°F. Remove with a slotted spoon and drain on the cooling rack. Repeat with the remaining pieces.

Serve warm with lemon wedges.

INGREDIENTS

2 Tbsp sesame oil

2 Tbsp canola oil

¾ cup toasted sunflower seeds,
   plus extra to serve

1 Tbsp grated fresh ginger

¼ cup soy sauce

3 Tbsp rice wine vinegar

¼ block silken soft tofu (about 3 oz)

Salt

1 lb green beans, stem ends trimmed

Green Bean Salad with Creamy Sunflower Seeds *Serves 4 to 6*

Biwa serves this nutty, gingery salad only in the summer, when green beans are at their peak, and guests eagerly await its arrival every year. But chef-owner Gabe Rosen says it's not just his customers who clamor for it, it's a staff favorite too. The recipe makes more dressing than you'll need for one salad, but it keeps for a couple of weeks in the refrigerator and is very versatile.

METHOD In a blender or food processor, combine the sesame oil, canola oil, sunflower seeds, ginger, soy sauce, and rice wine vinegar. Blend until very smooth and creamy. Break up the soft tofu with your hands, add it to the mixture, and blend until thoroughly combined. Season with salt to taste.

Bring a large pot of water to a boil and salt generously. Place a bowl of ice water near the stove. Add the green beans to the pot and cook for 2 minutes, or until just tender. Remove with a slotted spoon and immediately place in the ice water to stop the cooking. When completely cool, drain and pat dry.

Toss the green beans with a generous amount of dressing. Serve with sunflower seeds sprinkled on top.

CHRIS CARRIKER
Bluehour

WHEN BLUEHOUR OPENED in 2000, it represented the birth of a new kind of cool in Portland. Owner Bruce Carey had just closed the book on his seminal restaurant Zefiro, and Bluehour became, in effect, the next generation — the flag bearer for our dining scene's new chapter. It helped that it took root in the Pearl District, sort of a Northwest version of SoHo, where industrial warehouses were being transformed into hip boutiques, swanky art galleries, and expensive lofts. Bluehour was at the epicenter of it all.

Seventeen years later and Bluehour is still a symbol of Pearl District swank, the go-to spot for power meetings, date nights, and celebratory dinners. But at the same time, it serves as a neighborhood restaurant, a place with a fiercely loyal clientele, an easygoing happy hour, and a crowd-pleasing weekend brunch. Chef and meat maestro Chris Carriker helms a highly seasonal kitchen that pulls from the region's bounty with dishes like seared Oregon albacore with ice plant and herb emulsion, or locally raised Kurobuta pork with peaches, lentils, and mint. It's a menu that walks the line between fancy and approachable, just like the restaurant itself.

INGREDIENTS

2 cups all-purpose flour

2 cups pastry flour

2 Tbsp baking powder

1 tsp baking soda

2 tsp kosher salt

¾ cup (1 ½ sticks) frozen unsalted butter

6 oz frozen foie gras (see Note)

2 cups buttermilk

1 egg, beaten

1 Tbsp unsalted butter, melted

Foie Gras Biscuits

Makes 14

Substituting savory foie gras for half the butter in these mile-high biscuits has got to be one of the most genius ideas to ever grace a baking sheet. They're rich, they're flaky, and they're exactly what your plate of fried chicken and greens has been waiting for. Chef Chris Carriker says you can also add Tails and Trotters ham, two poached eggs, and foie gras hollandaise to make what he calls a "coma-inducing" eggs Benedict. "But even simply warmed with housemade preserves and butter will get the job done."

Note: Frozen foie gras can be purchased from online retailers such as D'Artagnan Foods and Hudson Valley Foie Gras.

METHOD Preheat oven to 425°F. Line a rimmed baking sheet with parchment paper.

In a large mixing bowl, whisk together the all-purpose flour, pastry flour, baking powder, baking soda, and salt. Grate the frozen butter and frozen foie gras on the large holes of a cheese grater or a food processor's grating disk. Add half the grated butter and half the foie gras into the flour mixture and toss until evenly combined. Add the remaining half and toss again.

Add the buttermilk and mix just until dough comes together (do not overmix or biscuits will be tough). Turn dough out onto a lightly floured surface and knead just a couple of times to form a cohesive mass. Roll or pat out into a large rectangle, fold it in on itself in thirds, and roll it out again. Fold into thirds one more time, then pat it out until it's 1 inch thick. Use a 2 ½-inch biscuit cutter to cut out the dough. Push the scraps together and cut out as many more as you can. You should have at least 14.

Arrange biscuits on the prepared baking sheet. Combine the egg and the melted butter in a small bowl, then brush the egg wash over the biscuits. Bake for 15 to 20 minutes, or until golden brown.

CIDER VINAIGRETTE

6 Tbsp extra-virgin olive oil (divided)

1 shallot, finely chopped

2 Tbsp apple brandy or apple cider

2 Tbsp cider vinegar

2 tsp Dijon mustard

1 tsp chopped fresh thyme

Salt and freshly ground black pepper

FONDUTA

1 Tbsp unsalted butter

1 Tbsp all-purpose flour

1 ¼ cups half-and-half

2 cups grated gruyère (about 5 oz)

Salt (optional)

SALAD

4 heads Belgian endive, leaves separated
   (or ½ head Treviso radicchio)

2 small heads frisée, leaves separated

2 Braeburn apples, cored and thinly
   sliced

1 cup store-bought candied walnuts

Salt and freshly ground black pepper

Belgian Endive and Frisée Salad with Apples, Fonduta, and Cider Vinaigrette *Serves 6*

It's a classic pairing: sweet, autumnal apples and slightly bitter cool-season greens. But it's the lush pool of gruyère *fonduta* on the bottom of each plate that sets this gorgeous salad apart. Every bite of bittersweet salad comes lightly slicked with the warm, tangy cheese sauce. It's truly a revelation.

CIDER VINAIGRETTE Heat 1 tablespoon of oil in a small sauté pan set over medium-high heat. Add the shallots and cook for 1 to 2 minutes, stirring occasionally, until tender. Add the apple brandy and reduce by half. Remove from heat and allow to cool.

In a medium bowl, combine the shallot mixture, vinegar, mustard, and thyme. Gradually whisk in the remaining 5 tablespoons of oil until emulsified. Season with salt and pepper to taste.

FONDUTA In a small saucepan, melt the butter over medium heat. Stir in the flour and cook for about 1 minute. Whisk in the half-and-half, a little at a time, letting the roux absorb the liquid before adding more. Allow to simmer gently over medium heat for 5 minutes, until thick enough to coat the back of a spoon.

Add the gruyère and whisk until the sauce is creamy and velvety smooth. Taste and season with a little salt, if desired. If it's too thick, add a bit of water. If it's too thin, add a little more cheese. (This can be made a day ahead and refrigerated. Rewarm in a saucepan set over medium-low heat to prevent the sauce from breaking.)

SALAD In a mixing bowl, toss the endive, frisée, and apples with just enough vinaigrette to coat. Divide the warm fonduta among each plate, top with salad, and sprinkle with candied walnuts. Season with salt and pepper to taste.

Bollywood Theater

Bollywood Theater

WHEN CHEF Troy MacLarty pulled up stakes in Berkeley to put down roots in Portland, he left one important thing behind: Indian street food. No longer could he head to Vik's Chaat Corner for *aloo tikki* potato patties and crispy, crackery *dahi papdi chaat* on his days off from Chez Panisse Café. So, being a chef, he did the only logical thing and opened up a *chaat* restaurant of his own.

First, though, he spent a good seven years earning a rep as one of the most talented farm-to-table chefs in town. But the call of the chutneys could not go unheeded, and in spring of 2012, after a year of serious R & D that included several weeks in India, he debuted Bollywood Theater on Northeast Alberta. Packed with a flea market's worth of Indian bric-a-brac and patinaed from ceiling to floor, Bollywood was a raging success from the get-go. People couldn't get enough of the innocent-looking yet flavor-crammed *kati* rolls, and *bhel puri* with its jumble of soft potatoes, crispy puffed rice, and crunchy peanuts, all lashed with tamarind and cilantro chutneys. Homesick Indians were begging him to take recipe requests and stocking up on *vada pav* "burgers" because they couldn't get them anywhere else. Two years later, MacLarty did the next logical thing—he opened a bigger outpost on Southeast Division and expanded the original to relieve its ever-present lines. It seems that in satisfying his cravings, he introduced the city to a whole new world of their own.

COCONUT MILK MARINADE

2 Tbsp canola oil

15 fresh curry leaves (see Note)

1 shallot, thinly sliced

1 serrano pepper, thinly sliced

13 ½ oz can coconut milk

¼ cup white wine vinegar

Salt

INDIAN SPICES

¼ cup canola oil

1 tsp yellow mustard seeds

1 tsp black mustard seeds

1 tsp cumin seeds

1 tsp nigella seeds (see Note)

BEETS

12 medium red beets

4 medium gold beets

2 Tbsp white wine vinegar

Salt

½ bunch fresh cilantro,
roughly chopped

Roasted Beets with Coconut Milk, Curry Leaves, and Indian Spices *Serves 6*

This has been one of the most popular, and vibrant, dishes on Bollywood Theater's menu ever since it opened. The rich marinade of spicy coconut curry livens up the earthy beets, making them absolutely crave-inducing. All the components can be made ahead of time, making it that much easier to get this exquisite side dish on the table, even on a busy weeknight.

Notes: You can find fresh curry leaves at specialty stores and Asian markets. They have a very unique flavor, almost like lemongrass, and are not at all related to curry powder. | Nigella seeds are tiny black seeds with a mild, oniony flavor. They are sometimes called kalonji *or nigella sativa. They look like black cumin, or* kala jeera, *but are different. Look for them at Indian markets or through online retailers.*

COCONUT MILK MARINADE Heat the oil in a medium sauté pan over medium heat and add the curry leaves, shallots, and serrano. Sauté until curry leaves are toasted and crispy, about 3 minutes. Add the coconut milk, bring to a simmer, and cook until reduced by one-quarter. Add white wine vinegar, taste, and adjust seasoning with salt. Allow to cool to room temperature. (Marinade can be made several days ahead and refrigerated.)

INDIAN SPICES Heat the oil in a small sauté pan over medium-low heat. Add the mustard seeds, cumin, and nigella seeds and cook until the cumin seeds are lightly browned. Allow to cool to room temperature. (Spices can be prepared several days ahead.)

BEETS Preheat oven to 400°F. Trim the beet tops and roots to within ½ inch of the bulb. Wrap the red and gold beets separately in foil and roast for 50 to 60 minutes, until tender. Peel and cut into 1-inch chunks, and place the red beets and gold beets in separate bowls. Toss each with a tablespoon of vinegar and generous pinch of salt. Allow to sit for 30 minutes. Divide coconut milk marinade between the bowls and allow beets to marinate for at least 30 minutes.

Divide the red beets among the plates and top with gold beets. Spoon Indian spices on top and sprinkle with chopped cilantro.

TURMERIC CURRY

1 Tbsp canola oil

3 cloves garlic, finely chopped

4 tsp chopped and peeled fresh
   turmeric (see Note)

2 cups heavy cream

¾ tsp paprika

½ tsp Kashmiri chili powder
   (see Note)

Freshly squeezed lemon juice

Salt

Grilled Broccoli with Fresh Turmeric Curry and Raisin Chutney *Serves 6*

It's easy to think Indian food is all saucy curries and rice, but at Bollywood Theater, chef-owner Troy MacLarty shows a different side of the cuisine, focusing on street food and vegetable-focused small plates like this incredibly flavorful side dish.

Notes: Fresh turmeric can be found at some specialty stores and Indian grocery stores. It's usually near the fresh ginger, looks a lot like it, and can be prepared in much the same way. Peel the outer skin and grate or chop. | Kashmiri chili powder is a deeply red, mildly spicy powder made from Kashmiri chiles. You can find it at Indian grocery stores. Or substitute a blend of equal parts cayenne and paprika.

TURMERIC CURRY Heat the oil in a medium sauté pan over medium heat. Add the garlic and sauté for 1 to 2 minutes, until aromatic. Add the turmeric and sauté for another minute. Add the cream, paprika, and chili powder, increase heat to medium-high, bring to a simmer, and cook until mixture is reduced to 1 cup. Taste and adjust seasoning with lemon juice and salt. Set aside. (Curry can be made several days ahead and refrigerated. Gently rewarm over low heat before using.)

CURRY OIL Heat oil in a small saucepan over medium heat. Add the curry powder and cayenne and cook for 1 minute. Remove from heat and strain through a coffee filter or cheesecloth. (Curry oil can be made several days ahead.)

CURRY OIL

¼ cup canola oil

½ tsp curry powder

¼ tsp cayenne

RAISIN CHUTNEY

¼ cup canola oil

¼ cup whole blanched almonds

¼ cup golden raisins

¼ cup dried currants

4 sprigs fresh cilantro, chopped

¼ cup Major Grey chutney, puréed
  if chunky

BROCCOLI

3 to 4 crowns broccoli, cut into
  3-inch florets (about 8 cups)

Canola oil

Kosher salt

RAISIN CHUTNEY Heat the oil in a small saucepan over medium-high heat. Add the almonds and fry for 5 to 7 minutes, or until toasted. Remove with a slotted spoon, drain on paper towels, and allow to cool before chopping.

Place raisins and currants in a small bowl and cover with boiling water. Allow to sit for about 30 seconds, or until plump. Drain.

In a mixing bowl, combine the raisins and currants, chopped almonds, cilantro, and chutney. (The raisin chutney can be made several days ahead and refrigerated.)

BROCCOLI In a large bowl, toss broccoli with just enough canola oil to coat and sprinkle with salt. Preheat grill to high. Grill the broccoli in a grill basket, tossing often, or arrange directly on the grill and turn frequently with tongs, for about 12 minutes, or until tender and edges are crispy and blackened. (Alternatively, you can roast the broccoli. Arrange in an even layer on a baking sheet and roast in a 425°F oven for 20 to 25 minutes.)

ASSEMBLY Arrange the broccoli on a platter, top with raisin chutney and turmeric curry, and drizzle with a few teaspoons of curry oil.

Broder

AT BRODER, personal-size skillets of potato hash arrive on wooden boards lined with blue gingham napkins, their oven-hot handles slipped into tiny handmade potholders. Pancakes come shaped like golden pompoms and sunny-side-up eggs are always in perfect squares. It's all part of the restaurant's ample charm, which manages to delight without being the least bit twee. And with a Scandinavian-inspired breakfast and lunch menu that's as rock-solid delicious as they come, it's easy to see why Broder is always at the top of everyone's brunch list.

Restaurateur and entrepreneur Peter Bro has an eye for design and for creating concepts that feed more than our hunger, and Broder is proof positive. He opened the original location in 2007, and it immediately struck a chord for its fresh take on brunch and serious attention to welcoming details. It has since expanded to two other Portland outposts plus one offshoot in the recreational town of Hood River. Day after day, chefs Daniel Oseas and Burt Hissong keep diners lining up for puffy, round *aebleskiver* with bright lemon curd for dipping, or delicate *lefse* potato crepes filled with seasonal vegetables and fresh cheese, and snacky *bords* loaded with cured fish and meats, roasted vegetables, and rustic breads. With an aquavit-spiked Bloody Mary in one hand and a puffy pancake in the other, a morning at Broder is a good morning indeed.

Pictured: Aebleskiver with Lemon Curd

Aebleskiver with Lemon Curd *Serves 4 (makes about 36 aebleskiver)*

Broder's Nordic-inflected brunch menu meanders from potato hash with pickled beets, baked eggs, and smoked trout to open-faced sandwiches called *smørrbrød*. But it's the puffy, spherical, lemon- and cardamom-scented *aebleskiver* that are the most irresistible. If you don't have an *aebleskiver* pan, consider this recipe your marching orders.

LEMON CURD In a food processor, pulse the lemon zest and sugar until well combined. Add the butter and blend until the mixture is smooth. With the machine running, add the eggs, one at a time, and then the lemon juice, processing until incorporated.

Transfer mixture to a medium saucepan and set over low heat. Cook, whisking frequently, until the mixture is 175°F. Pour the hot lemon curd into a bowl and refrigerate until cold, at least 1 hour. (Lemon curd can be made several days ahead and refrigerated.)

LEMON CURD

Zest of 1 lemon

½ cup granulated sugar

6 Tbsp (¾ stick) unsalted butter,
  softened

3 large eggs

½ cup freshly squeezed lemon juice
  (about 4 lemons)

AEBLESKIVER

1 egg

¼ tsp pure vanilla extract

Zest of ½ lemon

3 Tbsp granulated sugar

4 Tbsp (½ stick) melted butter
  (divided)

1 ¼ cups all-purpose flour

2 ¾ tsp baking powder

¼ tsp ground cardamom or
  cinnamon

¼ tsp salt

1 cup whole milk

Powdered sugar, for serving

AEBLESKIVER Combine the egg, vanilla, and lemon zest in a mixing bowl. Add the sugar and whisk vigorously until mixture is light in color and doubles in volume, about 5 minutes. (Alternatively, you can do this in a stand mixer fitted with the whisk attachment.) Slowly mix in 2 tablespoons of the melted butter.

In a small bowl, sift together the flour, baking powder, cardamom or cinnamon, and salt. Alternate stirring the dry ingredients and the milk into the egg mixture, mixing just until combined.

Place an *aebleskiver* pan over medium-low heat. Set a small bowl of the remaining 2 tablespoons melted butter and a pastry brush near the stove. Heat the oven to 200°F and set a baking sheet inside to keep the finished *aebleskiver* warm until serving. When the pan is hot enough to make a drop of water sizzle, brush each cup lightly with melted butter and use a ladle to fill with batter up to slightly below the rim.

In about 1 ½ minutes, thin crusts will form on the bottoms of the *aebleskiver*, but the centers will still be wet. Insert a slender wood skewer or chopstick all the way through and push to gently rotate each *aebleskive* until about half the crust is above the cup rim and uncooked batter flows down into the cup. Cook until a crust starts to form on the bottom again, about 30 seconds. Use two skewers to rotate each *aebleskive* again, this time turning them all the way over to form a ball (it helps to make a more rounded ball if you turn them diagonally this time). Cook, turning occasionally with the skewer, for another 1 to 2 minutes, or until the balls are evenly browned and no longer moist in the center. (A skewer inserted into the center of the last ball should come out clean.) If balls start to get too brown, turn heat to low until they are cooked in the center. Lift cooked balls from the pan and keep warm. Repeat with remaining batter.

Arrange the *aebleskiver* on a serving platter or pile into bowls. Sprinkle with powdered sugar and serve with lemon curd on the side.

DANISH MARY MIX

1 ½ tsp whole black peppercorns

1 small bay leaf

½ tsp kosher salt

½ tsp dry dill weed

½ tsp freshly ground white pepper

¼ tsp cayenne

½ tsp ground cumin

½ tsp dry mustard powder

1 tsp celery salt

¼ tsp curry powder

½ tsp paprika

½ tsp ground coriander

½ tsp garlic powder

½ tsp onion powder

1 tsp brown sugar

Juice of 4 lemons (½ cup)

1 Tbsp Worcestershire sauce

1 Tbsp balsamic vinegar

1 Tbsp apple cider vinegar

1 Tbsp prepared horseradish

⅓ cup tomato paste

46 oz can tomato juice

CELERY-DILL RIM SALT

3 Tbsp kosher salt

1 ½ tsp celery salt

1 ½ tsp dry dill weed

DANISH MARY COCKTAIL

Lemon wedge

Celery-dill rim salt (see here)

Ice

2 oz Gamle Ode Dill Aquavit, gin, or vodka

½ cup Danish Mary mix (see here)

Cherry tomatoes and pickled vegetables, such as beets, cucumbers, cauliflower, and onions, for garnish

Broder Söder Danish Mary *Serves 1*

With over a dozen spices in its mix, plus dill-infused aquavit, it's no surprise Broder's Nordic take on the classic Bloody Mary is consistently ranked among the best in the city. The rim salt and mix will make enough for about 14 cocktails. If you're not planning to have a party, you can store the salt in an airtight container indefinitely and freeze the Danish Mary mix for up to six months.

DANISH MARY MIX In a spice grinder or with a mortar and pestle, crush the peppercorns, bay leaf, salt, and dill until finely ground.

In a small skillet set over medium heat, combine the white pepper, cayenne, cumin, mustard powder, celery salt, curry powder, paprika, and coriander. Heat, stirring, until lightly toasted, about 2 minutes. Transfer to a small bowl and mix in the ground spices, garlic powder, onion powder, and brown sugar.

In a pitcher or 4-cup container with a lid, whisk together the lemon juice, Worcestershire sauce, balsamic vinegar, apple cider vinegar, horseradish, tomato paste, and spice mixture. Whisk until fully incorporated. Stir in the tomato juice and whisk until well combined. Taste and add more horseradish, salt, pepper, and/or sugar if desired. Refrigerate until cold. (Store, refrigerated, for up to 1 week.)

CELERY-DILL RIM SALT Combine all the ingredients together and mix well. Store in an airtight container.

DANISH MARY COCKTAIL Moisten the rim of a pint glass with a lemon wedge. Dip the rim of the glass into the rim salt to coat. Fill the glass with ice, add aquavit, and top with ½ cup Danish Mary mix, or more to taste. Stir and garnish with a skewer of cherry tomatoes and pickled vegetables.

CARLO LAMAGNA & JEFFREY MORGENTHALER
Clyde Common

WITH ITS PARED-DOWN vibe, lofty space, open kitchen, and communal tables, Clyde Common set the tone for the new generation of Portland restaurants when it opened in 2007. Everything about it was effortlessly cool, like no one had to try very hard to be brilliant. Dining there made us all feel effortlessly cool by proxy, and Clyde was welcoming and gracious enough to indulge us. This is why, 10 years later, Portland still adores Clyde with the devotion of a first love. And situated as it is downtown, next door to the similarly cool Ace Hotel, it's just as beloved by out-of-towners too.

Of course, that cool factor would be nothing without the food and drinks to back it up, and Clyde has consistently delivered year after year with super-seasonal shared plates and craft cocktails that consistently raise the bar not just in Portland, but across the nation. If you've

had a barrel-aged cocktail, you can thank bar manager Jeffrey Morgenthaler, who has led the bar program to several James Beard Award nominations and made national press more times than we can count. Three years ago, executive chef Carlo Lamagna took over the kitchen and energized the menu with Asian inflections and fun, family-style feasts. Owners Nate Tilden (one of the city's most prolific, and successful, restaurateurs) and respected barman Matt Piacentini seem to operate by the philosophy "hire good people and let them do their thing." Clearly it's a philosophy that works.

Pictured: Grilled Trout with Scallop Mousse and Citrus-Pink Peppercorn Vinaigrette & Bourbon Renewal

Grilled Trout with Scallop Mousse and Citrus-Pink Peppercorn Vinaigrette *Serves 8*

Scallop mousse just sounds so fancy, but this gorgeous whole-fish preparation is actually incredibly easy. If you're looking for a special dinner without too much effort, this is it — especially if you ask your fishmonger to debone and butterfly the trout for you. You will have extra scallop mousse left over, but it's fabulous spread on toast and grilled under the broiler. Add a fried or poached egg and call it lunch.

Note: Be sure to get natural, dry-pack scallops, which means they haven't been soaked in a wet preservative mixture. The added moisture from the preservative will turn the scallops into soup when puréed. Natural, dry-pack scallops will be light tan in color, not white, and will be labeled "no added preservatives."

CITRUS VINAIGRETTE In a blender, combine the orange, grapefruit, and lemon juices, honey, pepper, and mustard. Blend on low for 20 seconds, then slowly add the oil in a thin, steady stream until incorporated and the mixture is emulsified. Season with salt to taste.

STUFFED TROUT In a food processor, combine the scallops, egg, and orange zest. Pulse until a chunky paste forms. With the motor running, slowly drizzle in the cream through the feed tube until fully incorporated and the mixture is fluffy. Season with salt and pepper to taste. (To test seasoning, cook a small amount of the mixture in a sauté pan and taste. Adjust as needed.)

Open up the trout on a work surface. Season the flesh generously with salt. Sprinkle with pepper. Add 3 tablespoons of the scallop mousse to each trout and spread into an even layer. Close the fish back up and season the skin with salt and pepper. Coat with oil.

CITRUS VINAIGRETTE

½ cup freshly squeezed orange juice

¼ cup freshly squeezed grapefruit juice

¼ cup freshly squeezed lemon juice

2 Tbsp honey

1 Tbsp freshly ground pink peppercorns

1 Tbsp Dijon mustard

1 ½ cups vegetable oil

Salt

STUFFED TROUT

1 lb dry-pack bay or sea scallops
  (see Note)

1 egg

2 Tbsp orange zest

1 cup heavy cream

Salt and freshly ground black pepper

4 (12 oz) whole rainbow trout, deboned,
  butterflied, and pinbones removed

Canola oil

1 bunch radishes, sliced

1 large bulb fennel, sliced

2 cups fresh Italian parsley leaves (optional)

Preheat grill to medium-hot. Grill the trout for 10 minutes on each side until mousse is cooked through (internal temperature of about 145°F). Alternatively, you can pan-roast the fish: preheat oven to 425°F. Set a large sauté pan over medium-high heat and add enough oil to generously coat the bottom. Add the fish and allow to cook until seared and golden brown, about 5 minutes. Turn and cook the other side for another 5 minutes. Transfer to the oven to finish cooking, about 10 minutes more.

Combine the radishes, fennel, and parsley in a bowl and toss with just enough vinaigrette to coat. Taste and adjust seasoning if needed.

Divide the radish salad among plates. Cut each trout in half and set on top. Spoon more vinaigrette over the trout and serve.

INGREDIENTS

1 ½ oz bourbon

¾ oz freshly squeezed lemon juice

½ oz crème de cassis

¼ oz rich simple syrup (see Note)

Dash of Angostura bitters

Ice

Lemon wheel, for garnish

Bourbon Renewal

Serves 1

One of Jeffrey Morgenthaler's most popular cocktails at Clyde Common combines oaky bourbon with bright lemon and just a touch of sweet cassis.

Note: To make rich simple syrup, combine 1 cup granulated sugar and ½ cup water in a medium saucepan set over medium-high heat. Bring to a simmer and cook about 3 minutes, until sugar is completely dissolved and mixture is syrupy. Cool completely before using. Syrup will keep refrigerated for several weeks.

METHOD Combine the bourbon, lemon juice, crème de cassis, simple syrup, bitters, and ice in a cocktail shaker. Shake vigorously for 15 seconds. Strain into a short tumbler filled with ice. Garnish with a lemon wheel.

Clyde Common

The Country Cat

IT'S NO SMALL FEAT to open an ambitious, highly seasonal, nose-to-tail restaurant miles from the city center. But chefs Adam and Jackie Sappington took the leap anyway, opening The Country Cat in the sleepy Montavilla neighborhood way back in 2007. They left one of Portland's most acclaimed restaurants, Wildwood, to launch a place of their own where they could merge their love of Heartland cuisine with the flavors and ingredients of the Northwest. That was 10 years ago, a lifetime in restaurant years, and The Country Cat still has lines out the door, with a following that goes well beyond city, county, or even state borders. They've written a James Beard–nominated cookbook, opened a neighboring event space, and, even

more impressive, launched a spin-off location at Portland International Airport, where fellow chefs Instagram their eggs Benedict before takeoff. Yes, it's airport food and it's that good.

But it's all in a day's work for the Sappingtons, who cut no corners whether they're serving jet-lagged travelers in an airport terminal or jet-setting one-percenters at a big-ticket gala. Adam's fried chicken takes three days to prepare. Jackie's biscuits rise a mile high. And their menu never, ever rests on its Midwestern laurels, as new dishes come and go with the seasons.

½ cup extra-virgin olive oil (divided)

12 large asparagus spears, ends trimmed

Salt

6 radishes, very thinly sliced

2 scallions, very thinly sliced

Zest of 2 lemons, plus juice if desired

1 bunch fresh mint leaves, torn

6 oz feta

¼ cup white vermouth vinegar, moscato vinegar, or apple cider vinegar

1 bunch watercress, roots trimmed

Warm Asparagus, Scallion, and Radish Salad with Lemon Zest and Crumbled Feta *Serves 4*

Although The Country Cat is known for rib-sticking, nose-to-tail dishes, chefs Adam and Jackie Sappington have a deft hand with vegetables as well. This light, composed salad is a simple and delicious celebration of spring. At the restaurant they use Unio brand vermouth vinegar, which you can buy online, but it can be substituted with moscato vinegar or apple cider vinegar.

METHOD Heat ¼ cup of the olive oil in a large sauté pan over medium heat. Add the asparagus and season with salt. Add about ¼ cup water and cover. Cook until tender, about 3 minutes. Remove the lid and cook the asparagus until the water has evaporated and the asparagus begins to glaze with the olive oil.

In a mixing bowl, combine the radishes, scallions, lemon zest, mint, and feta. Add the vinegar and remaining ¼ cup of olive oil and toss. Season with salt and a squeeze of lemon if desired.

Divide watercress among four salad plates. Top each with three stalks of asparagus. Divide the radish and onion salad among the plates. Season to taste and add a squeeze of lemon if desired.

TOPPING

3 Tbsp unsalted butter, plus more for greasing the pan

⅓ cup packed brown sugar

2 Bosc pears, peeled, cored, and cut into eighths

CAKE

½ cup golden raisins

3 Tbsp dark rum

1 ¼ cups plus 1 Tbsp all-purpose flour

1 ½ tsp baking powder

½ tsp baking soda

2 ¼ tsp ground cinnamon

¾ tsp freshly grated nutmeg

¼ tsp salt

¾ cup (1 ½ sticks) unsalted butter, softened

1 ½ cups granulated sugar

3 eggs

¾ cup pumpkin purée

VANILLA WHIPPED CREAM

2 cups heavy cream

3 Tbsp powdered sugar

1 ½ tsp pure vanilla extract or vanilla bean paste

Pumpkin Upside-Down Cake with Caramelized Pears *Serves 8*

In pastry chef Jackie Sappington's hands, the classic caramel-soaked cake gets an autumnal makeover. Pears stand in for the usual pineapple, and the tender cake is blended with rum raisins, cinnamon, nutmeg, and pumpkin purée.

TOPPING Set a 9-inch metal cake pan over medium-low heat. Add the butter and brown sugar and heat, stirring, until melted and combined. Remove from heat and arrange the pears in a circle. Lightly grease the sides of the pan with butter.

CAKE Preheat oven to 350°F. In a small bowl, combine the raisins and rum and set aside.

In a medium mixing bowl, combine the flour, baking powder, baking soda, cinnamon, nutmeg, and salt.

Using a stand mixer or hand mixer, cream the butter and sugar on high speed until fluffy, about 2 minutes. Scrape down the sides of the bowl and add the eggs, one at a time, beating well after each addition.

With the mixer on low, add half the dry ingredients, the pumpkin purée, and then the remaining dry ingredients. Add the raisin and rum mixture.

Spread the batter evenly over the pears, making sure they are all covered. Place on the middle rack of the oven and bake for 30 to 40 minutes, or until a toothpick inserted in the center comes out clean.

Allow the cake to rest for 5 minutes, then run a knife around the edges of the pan to loosen the cake. Place a serving platter or large plate over the cake and flip the pan over. Tap the pan to release the fruit, then gently lift the pan off the cake. (If any fruit remains stuck to the pan, just remove it and place it on top of the cake.)

VANILLA WHIPPED CREAM Using a stand mixer or hand mixer fitted with the whisk attachment, or by hand, whisk the cream, sugar, and vanilla extract or paste until soft peaks form. Cut cake into slices and serve with vanilla whipped cream.

GREGORY GOURDET

Departure

WITH ITS SUPER-SLEEK modernism and nary a trace of Portland-esque plaid and taxidermy, the swank restaurant atop downtown's most luxe hotel — The Nines — is widely known to be the least "Portland" restaurant in Portland. Yet the chef at the helm embodies everything we love about this city's restaurant scene. Gregory Gourdet is deeply talented (a *Top Chef* finalist, no less), unafraid to experiment, and the living embodiment of collaboration. He is, in many ways, the glue that keeps the industry working together, whether he's pitching in at a fellow chef's event or creating one of his own.

He brings that same generosity of spirit to his menu at Departure. From small plates to large, he taps into the world of Asian cuisines using ingredients and flavors from Chinese, Japanese, Korean, and Vietnamese traditions.

The result is exquisitely prepared bites that pop with flavor and are perfect accompaniments to the bar's lineup of bold cocktails. Under Gourdet's leadership, Departure is a place where people can unwind with a fancy cocktail and a bite of sushi from the rooftop deck or go all out and celebrate with a full Peking duck dinner during the holidays. As high-design as it is, it welcomes all comers, and Gourdet wouldn't have it any other way.

Pictured: Vietnamese Duck Curry

Vietnamese Duck Curry *Serves 4*

Departure chef Gregory Gourdet uses all parts of the duck in this incredibly rich and flavorful curry, but to make it more accessible for home cooks, this version uses store-bought stock and confit. Can't find the confit? Don't fret. The sauce is so delicious, you can serve it with just about anything, even tofu. Just be sure to serve it with enough crusty bread or steamed rice to soak it all up.

Notes: Some specialty and gourmet grocers carry duck breasts and duck leg confit in the butcher department or deli or freezer section. Look for duck stock in the freezer section, too, or check the soup aisle for More Than Gourmet brand duck and chicken stock base (also available through online retailers). You can also special-order the meats from your butcher. In Oregon, any retailer that works with Nicky USA can source the duck breast and duck leg confit for you. | Cutting taro can make your hands itch. If your skin is sensitive, wear gloves.

CURRY In a blender or food processor, combine the garlic, lemongrass, onions, chile, ginger, curry paste, salt, and peppercorns. Blend or process until very smooth.

Heat the oil in a medium pot set over medium heat. Add the curry mixture and cook 10 minutes, or until the color darkens and flavors deepen. Stir in the coconut milk and duck stock. Bring to a simmer over medium-high heat and cook for 1 hour, or until reduced by half. Season with sugar and fish sauce.

CURRY

10 small cloves garlic, chopped

4 stalks lemongrass, pounded
and very thinly sliced

2 onions, chopped

1 Fresno chile pepper or
jalapeño pepper

3-inch piece fresh ginger, peeled
and thinly sliced

2 Tbsp Thai red curry paste

1 Tbsp salt

1 tsp whole black peppercorns

¼ cup vegetable oil

3 (13 ½ oz) cans coconut milk

5 cups duck stock (see Note)

1 Tbsp granulated sugar

2 Tbsp fish sauce (such as
Red Boat)

ASSEMBLY

1 medium taro root (see Note)

2 Tbsp extra-virgin olive oil (divided)

2 duck breasts

Salt and freshly ground black pepper

2 confit duck legs (see Note)

24 fresh Thai basil leaves, plus
more to garnish

1 bunch scallions, sliced

Artisan bread or steamed rice,
to serve

ASSEMBLY Preheat oven to 425°F. Peel the taro root and cut into medium dice. (You should have 3 cups.) Arrange on a rimmed baking sheet, toss with 1 tablespoon of the olive oil, and roast for 15 minutes, or until tender.

Using a sharp knife, score the skin of the duck breast diagonally in both directions to create a diamond pattern (don't cut the flesh). Season with salt and pepper. Heat the remaining tablespoon of oil in a medium sauté pan set over medium-high heat. Add the duck breasts, skin side down, and sear until the skin is golden brown and crisp, about 5 minutes (meat won't be fully cooked). Remove from heat and set aside to cool. Slice ¼ inch thick. (Refrigerate or freeze the flavorful duck fat for another use, like roasting potatoes or vegetables.)

Add the duck leg confit and taro root to the curry and simmer until warmed through. Add the duck breast and simmer for about 5 minutes, until the meat is medium-rare.

To serve, fold in the Thai basil. Divide the duck between four bowls and cover with curry sauce. Garnish with sliced scallions and Thai basil and serve with warm bread or steamed rice.

DRESSING

1 cup white miso

3 Tbsp freshly squeezed lemon juice

3 Tbsp rice wine vinegar

1 Tbsp maple syrup

½ small shallot, chopped

1-inch piece fresh ginger, peeled
  and chopped

Zest of ½ lemon

Sea salt

Power Greens Salad with Root Vegetables and Miso Dressing *Serves 4 to 6*

We know chef Gregory Gourdet as the talent behind Departure, but we also know him as a committed ultrarunner, who fuels his 30-mile runs through Portland's Forest Park with clean-eating, power-packed dishes like this. It's made with four kinds of greens, including peppery Asian mizuna, which can be found at farmers' markets, specialty grocers, and Asian markets. The pickled lotus root not only looks beautiful, but adds a refreshing crunch, while the jalapeño oil enhances the salad with warm heat.

Notes: You can find fresh lotus root and shiso leaves at Asian markets. | To make jalapeño oil, gently simmer two sliced jalapeño peppers with ½ cup olive oil for 10 minutes. Remove from heat and set aside to steep for 1 hour. Strain. Infused oil will keep up to a month refrigerated. | Toasted hemp seeds are available at natural food stores such as Whole Foods.

DRESSING In a blender or food processor, combine the miso, lemon juice, vinegar, maple syrup, shallots, ginger, and lemon zest. Blend or process until smooth and creamy. Season with salt to taste. (Dressing will keep up to 1 week refrigerated.)

PICKLED LOTUS ROOT Using a mandoline, slice the lotus root as thinly as possible (you should have about 1 cup). Place in a nonreactive bowl.

In a small saucepan, bring the vinegar, sugar, and chile to a simmer. Remove from heat and pour over the lotus root. Cover with parchment paper or plastic to submerge in the brine. Let cool to room temperature, then refrigerate overnight. (Lotus root will keep up to 1 week refrigerated.)

PICKLED LOTUS ROOT

1 small fresh lotus root, peeled
  (see Note)
1 cup rice wine vinegar
½ cup granulated sugar
1 red chile, sliced (remove
  seeds for less heat)

SALAD

½ bunch collard greens, stems
  removed and leaves chopped
  (about 2 cups)
½ bunch kale, stems removed and
  leaves chopped (about 2 cups)
1 bunch spinach, stems removed and
  leaves chopped (about 2 cups)
2 cups mizuna
1 yellow beet, peeled and thinly sliced

1 large carrot, peeled and thinly
  sliced
½ red onion, sliced
6 shiso leaves (see Note)
1 Tbsp jalapeño oil, or to taste
  (see Note)
¼ cup toasted hemp seeds, for
  garnish (see Note)
¼ cup edible flowers, for garnish
  (optional)

SALAD In a large bowl, combine the collards, kale, spinach, mizuna, beets, carrots, and onions. Toss with just enough miso dressing to coat. Fold in shiso leaves and season with jalapeño oil. Garnish with pickled lotus, toasted hemp seeds, and edible flowers.

DOC | Yakuza

RESTAURATEUR Dayna McErlean has a knack for creating neighborhood joints that rock. She runs three restaurants, all located within a block of each other, in deeply residential Northeast Portland. But though they're tucked away amid bungalows, for years they've been bringing in diners from all quadrants with their sheer conviviality and enthusiastic commitment to Northwest-grown food.

At shoebox-size DOC, named in honor of Italy's strict quality control labels, diners walk through the open kitchen to take their seats, getting an up-close-and-personal glimpse of the super-fresh produce and pasture-raised meats that chef Brian Christopher uses to craft his Italian-accented menu. He packs a wallop of ambition into this tiny space, with seasonally driven dishes like Roman gnocchi with bacon, corn, jalapeño, and ricotta salata.

But nine-year-old DOC can't completely contain his creativity, so he oversees the menu at Nonna, its sister restaurant next door. The cozy, tavern-like space is the perfect setting for his heartier dishes, like bucatini puttanesca with fresh tuna, and belly-filling weekend brunch dishes like fermented waffles, fried chicken, and fennel pollen syrup.

Down the street at Yakuza, chef Caleb Vasquez's food takes a 180-degree turn, with a Japanese-inspired menu of sushi, sashimi, and one of the most acclaimed burgers in Portland—a mix of Kobe-style beef, *togarashi*, shoestring fries, and (of all things) goat cheese. It's a perfect example of Yakuza's playful, and highly successful, take on Japanese flavors. At 11 years old, Yakuza is still going strong, its generous happy hour and backyard oasis making it feel like Portland's home away from home.

1 (1 ½ lb) lamb rack (8 ribs), fat cap trimmed

Salt and freshly ground black pepper

4 Tbsp grapeseed oil (divided)

2 cups (1 pint) Padrón peppers

2 slightly underripe avocados, halved and
   cut crosswise into 1-inch-thick slices

2 ripe peaches, sliced 1-inch thick

1 lemon

Roasted Rack of Lamb with Peaches, Padróns, and Avocado *Serves 4*

This late-summer dish from DOC is as easy and breezy as the season itself. The chops are simply seasoned and quickly pan-roasted, then served alongside a gorgeous sauté of mildly spicy Padrón peppers, sweet peaches, and avocado slices, browned to bring out their savory side.

METHOD Preheat oven to 450°F. Split lamb rack into four 2-rib chops and season each with salt and pepper.

Heat 2 tablespoons of oil in a large sauté pan set over medium-high heat. Add the lamb chops and sear on one side for about 3 minutes, until browned. Turn the chops over and place the pan in the oven. Roast for 7 minutes, until medium-rare.

Meanwhile, heat the remaining 2 tablespoons of oil in a large sauté pan over medium-high heat. Add the peppers and avocados and sauté until browned all over. Season with salt to taste.

Transfer the peppers and avocados to a large bowl. Add the peaches and season with lemon juice and salt to taste. Toss gently to coat. Divide among four dishes, set two chops on top of each, and serve.

PANCAKE BATTER

1 ½ cups all-purpose flour

2 Tbsp granulated sugar

2 tsp baking powder

½ tsp baking soda

½ tsp salt

2 eggs

1 ¼ cups buttermilk

2 Tbsp vegetable oil

1 cup firmly packed finely
   chopped kimchi

1 Tbsp gochugaru (see Note)

1 Tbsp paprika

Okonomiyaki with Wild Mushrooms *Serves 4 to 6*

These savory pancakes called *okonomiyaki* are a staple street food in Japan, where they're usually served with a variety of vegetables and seafood or meat either cooked right in the batter or served on top. The fillings range depending on the region, and in some places you can customize them yourself. This version from Yakuza makes use of our abundance of wild mushrooms for a particularly Northwest take.

Note: Gochugaru is a Korean spice made of coarsely ground red peppers. It's commonly used to make kimchi and can be found at Asian markets.

PANCAKE BATTER Sift the flour, sugar, baking powder, baking soda, and salt into a large bowl. Make a well in the middle and add the eggs. Whisk the eggs to break them up, then add the buttermilk and oil. Whisk batter until smooth. Stir in the chopped kimchi, *gochugaru*, and paprika. Set aside.

SPICY MAYO Whisk the mayonnaise, Sriracha, and lemon juice together in a small bowl. Add salt to taste. (This can be made a week ahead and refrigerated.)

SPICY MAYO

1 cup mayonnaise

¼ cup Sriracha

2 tsp freshly squeezed
 lemon juice

Salt

ASSEMBLY

10 to 12 large dry-pack sea scallops

2 to 4 Tbsp grapeseed oil or other
 high-heat oil (divided)

3 Tbsp unsalted butter

2 cups chopped, firmly packed
 mushrooms (such as shiitake with
 stems removed, porcini, or morels)

Salt and freshly ground black pepper

1 small head frisée

2 scallions, thinly sliced

¼ cup fresh radish sprouts or other
 microgreens, for garnish

ASSEMBLY Preheat oven to 200°F.

Rinse the scallops in a strainer under cold running water. Remove the foot (the small strip of flesh located on the side; the foot is too chewy when cooked).

Heat a cast-iron skillet over high heat until evenly hot. Reduce heat to medium-low and add 1 tablespoon of oil, tilting the pan to coat. Using a ¼-cup ladle, pour the batter into the pan to make 3-inch-diameter pancakes. Cook for about 1 minute, until golden brown on the bottom. Flip and cook for another minute, until the pancakes are cooked through. Wrap the cooked pancakes loosely in foil and place in the warm oven. Repeat with the remaining batter, using more oil as necessary.

Set a small sauté pan over medium heat. Add the butter, the mushrooms, and a pinch of salt. Sauté until mushrooms begin to soften, about 3 minutes. Reduce heat to low and keep warm.

Heat the remaining 1 tablespoon oil in a large sauté pan set over high heat. Season the scallops with salt and pepper. When oil is hot, add the scallops and sear for 1 ½ minutes, until browned. Turn and cook the other side until browned, about 1 ½ minutes more. Remove from heat.

Arrange each plate with a bed of frisée leaves. Set a couple pancakes on top. Add a dollop of spicy mayo, then divide the scallions, mushrooms, and scallops between each dish. Garnish with radish sprouts.

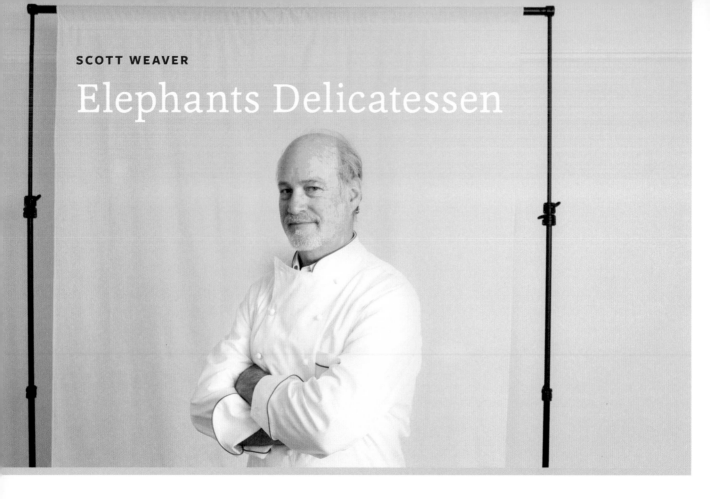

SCOTT WEAVER
Elephants Delicatessen

PORTLAND NATIVES (of a certain age) remember a completely different dining landscape than the one we have now, a time when it was *de rigueur* for restaurants to serve produce from a can rather than a local farm. And they remember when a little delicatessen opened up in 1979 and changed everything. Elephants Delicatessen was the Northwest version of Manhattan's Silver Palate, a place that brought a European sensibility to the pragmatic Northwest, stocking shelves with artisanal specialty goods from France and Italy and giving new meaning to the word "gourmet." This is where Portland got its first taste of fresh pasta, pesto sauce, chocolate truffles, and cheeses from around the world, and our taste buds have never been the same since.

Executive chef–owner Scott Weaver has been there almost from the beginning. He joined the team in 1983 at the tender age of 25, after being mentored by James Beard himself and earning his stripes as Portland's youngest head chef when he took over the Norton House, one of Portland's first farm-to-table restaurants. In his 34-year tenure, he's built Elephants into a Portland icon with eight locations and an extraordinarily busy catering staff, and developed over 4,000 recipes that consistently keep up with the changing times. The original Northwest location is still jam-packed with people picking up lunch or dinner to go or sitting down to something hot from the grill. And though the shelves still groan with specialty goods, these days they're more likely made in the Northwest than flown in from abroad. It's an evolution indicative of our dining scene and one that has a lot to do with Elephants itself.

ELEPHANTS MARINARA SAUCE

3 Tbsp extra-virgin olive oil

1 small carrot, diced

2 cloves garlic, finely chopped

½ tsp finely chopped fresh rosemary

14 oz can whole tomatoes

3 Tbsp tomato purée

Several fresh basil leaves, whole

Salt and freshly ground black pepper

PROSCIUTTO-TOMATO CREAM SAUCE

1 oz prosciutto, cut into strips

½ cup Elephants marinara sauce
  (see here)

¼ cup heavy cream

Salt and freshly ground white pepper

ASSEMBLY

2 Tbsp extra-virgin olive oil (divided)

1 lb extra-large tail-on shrimp
  (26/30 count), peeled and deveined

4 cups arugula

Salt and freshly ground black pepper

Prosciutto, for garnish

Shrimp with Arugula and Prosciutto-Tomato Cream Sauce *Serves 4*

Elephants' marinara sauce is a building block for many of its dishes. Here it is simmered with savory prosciutto and spiked with cream, transforming it into sheer decadence. Portlanders know it well as the sauce for one of the restaurant's most popular take-and-bake penne casseroles, but this dish offers a more refined presentation, with sautéed shrimp and wilted arugula.

ELEPHANTS MARINARA SAUCE Heat the oil in a large heavy-bottomed saucepan over medium-high heat. Add the carrots and sauté until tender, about 8 minutes. Add the garlic and rosemary and sauté until fragrant, about 1 minute more. Add the canned tomatoes and tomato purée, stirring to scrape up any browned bits. Stir in the basil leaves. Bring to a simmer, reduce heat to medium, and cook for 10 minutes, breaking up the tomatoes with the back of a spoon as they cook. Season with salt and pepper to taste. Set aside ½ cup. Store the remainder in the refrigerator for up to 3 days or freeze for longer storage.

PROSCIUTTO-TOMATO CREAM SAUCE In a saucepan over medium heat, combine the prosciutto and marinara sauce. Bring to a simmer and cook for 3 to 4 minutes. Stir in the cream and simmer for 1 minute. Season with salt and pepper to taste.

ASSEMBLY Heat 1 tablespoon of oil in a large sauté pan over medium-high heat. Add shrimp and sauté for 2 to 3 minutes, until opaque. Transfer to the sauce and simmer for a minute to warm through. Remove from heat.

Heat the remaining 1 tablespoon of oil in the sauté pan over medium-high heat. Add arugula and cook for a few seconds, until wilted. Season with salt and pepper and divide among plates. Place the shrimp and sauce on top of the arugula and garnish with a few prosciutto strips.

HAZELNUT BUTTER

¼ cup unsalted butter

½ cup chopped hazelnuts

1 tsp freshly squeezed lemon juice

Pinch of salt

CABBAGE, FENNEL, AND FRISÉE SAUTÉ

2 Tbsp extra-virgin olive oil

1 ½ tsp yellow mustard seeds

1 small bulb fennel, thinly sliced

½ cup thinly sliced green cabbage

½ tsp garlic powder

½ tsp ground turmeric

Salt and freshly ground black pepper

2 cups frisée leaves

ASSEMBLY

4 fillets wild salmon (about 1 ¼ lb)

Salt and freshly ground black pepper

Grilled Wild Salmon with Hazelnut Butter and Cabbage, Fennel, and Frisée Sauté *Serves 4*

One of the most popular items from Elephants' extensive catering menu, this elegant dish blends two of the Pacific Northwest's most prized ingredients: wild salmon and hazelnuts. If you have any hazelnut butter left over, try it on top of roasted vegetables or other meats, or stirred into a whole-grain pilaf.

HAZELNUT BUTTER Heat the butter in a large sauté pan over medium heat, until the milk solids are just starting to brown (watch carefully to make sure they don't get too dark and burn). Add the hazelnuts and sauté for 1 to 2 minutes, until lightly toasted. Remove from heat and add the lemon juice and salt.

CABBAGE, FENNEL, AND FRISÉE SAUTÉ Heat the olive oil in a large sauté pan over medium-high heat. Add the mustard seeds and sauté until lightly toasted and beginning to pop. Add the fennel and cabbage and sauté until tender, about 4 minutes.

Add the garlic powder, turmeric, and salt and pepper to taste. Sauté for about 4 minutes more. Add the frisée to the pan and cook just long enough to wilt. Remove from heat but keep warm.

ASSEMBLY Sprinkle both sides of each fillet with salt and pepper. Preheat grill to medium-hot. Grill the fish, skin side down, for 4 to 6 minutes, or until it flakes easily with a fork. (Cooking time will depend on the size of your fish fillets. Alternatively, you can broil or pan-roast the salmon.)

Divide the warm cabbage sauté among four serving dishes. Set a salmon fillet on top, spoon hazelnut butter over each fillet, and serve.

SARAH SCHAFER

Irving Street Kitchen

WHEN NEWS CAME that three big-time San Francisco restaurateurs with Wolfgang Puck pedigrees were going to open a restaurant in Portland—with a chef who was the executive sous at New York's famed Gramercy Tavern and Eleven Madison Park—expectations were pretty high to say the least. And it's a testament to their business acumen and chef Sarah Schafer's cooking prowess that the team didn't disappoint.

Tucked behind a loading dock in a former warehouse in the Pearl District, seven-year-old Irving Street Kitchen sports a high-end country glam that seems a fitting match to the globe-trotting, Southern-inspired menu. Schafer's buttermilk fried chicken and double-smoked pork chop are legendary, but alongside such Dixie delights are dishes like halibut with lobster mushrooms and sorrel crème fraîche or chorizo and squid ink risotto. The ever-popular brunch menu follows suit, with chicken and waffles and buttermilk biscuit Benedicts on the same page as Moroccan poached eggs. Though Schafer and her menu have serious chops, there's an air of playful hospitality, too, with Oregon wines on tap, butterscotch puddings to go, and a happy hour so good and cheap, you start planning your days around it. It's clear that Schafer, a tireless fundraiser for nonprofits like Share Our Strength, is just as committed to making Irving Street Kitchen a valued part of the community as she is about making it a dining destination. She may not be a hometown girl, but she's certainly made her new home a better place.

Pictured: Moroccan Poached Eggs
with Garlic-Rubbed Levain

Moroccan Poached Eggs with Garlic-Rubbed Levain *Serves 6*

One of the best things about this gorgeous dish, aside from its evocative "spice route" flavors, is that you can make the sauce ahead of time. Simply rewarm it while you poach some eggs and toast some bread, and you have a restaurant-worthy breakfast in minutes.

Notes: Black limes are essentially dried limes and are often used in Persian cooking for their complex, sour flavor. They can be found in Middle Eastern grocery stores. To crush, just pound the lime on a kitchen counter. | Ras el hanout is a Moroccan spice blend that usually has cinnamon, ginger, allspice, and cloves plus savory spices like cumin, coriander, and cayenne. You can find it at Middle Eastern grocery stores. Every purveyor makes it a little different; Chef Schafer prefers the version sold through Kalustyans.com.

MOROCCAN SAUCE Heat the oil in a medium saucepan set over medium-high heat. Add the onions, leeks, carrots, and fennel and sauté for about 10 minutes, until tender. Add the curry, cumin, black lime, cinnamon, and cayenne. Cook, stirring, for about 1 minute, or until fragrant. Add the tomatoes and vegetable stock, bring to a boil over high heat, reduce to medium, and simmer for 1 hour.

Discard any large pieces of lime and pass the sauce through a food mill or purée with an immersion blender. Stir in the cream. Taste and adjust seasoning with salt and pepper. Keep warm if using right away, or transfer to an airtight container and refrigerate for up to 1 week.

MOROCCAN SAUCE

1 Tbsp extra-virgin olive oil

½ onion, sliced

½ leek, white and light green parts, sliced

1 carrot, peeled and sliced

1 small bulb fennel, sliced

1 Tbsp curry powder

½ tsp ground cumin

1 black lime, crushed (see Note)

Dash of ground cinnamon

Dash of cayenne, plus more to taste

2 (28 oz) cans San Marzano tomatoes

½ cup vegetable stock

2 Tbsp heavy cream

Salt and freshly ground black pepper

ASSEMBLY

1 cup panko or breadcrumbs

1 tsp ras el hanout (see Note)

2 Tbsp extra-virgin olive oil

6 (1-inch-thick) slices levain or sourdough bread

1 large clove garlic

1 Tbsp distilled white vinegar

12 eggs

3 Tbsp chopped fresh cilantro, to serve

ASSEMBLY Preheat oven to 350°F. In a small bowl, toss the panko, ras el hanout, and oil together. Spread on a rimmed baking sheet and toast for 10 minutes, or until golden brown. (This can be made ahead and stored in an airtight container.)

Preheat broiler. Grill the bread under the broiler until slightly charred. Rub each piece once or twice with the raw garlic clove (don't rub it too many times or it will be too garlicky).

Bring a large skillet of water to a steady simmer over medium-high heat and add the vinegar. Crack an egg into a ramekin or cup. Slowly tip the egg into the water, whites first. Repeat with the remaining eggs, or cook them in batches if your pan is not big enough. When whites begin to set, use a rubber spatula to gently move them around to prevent them from sticking. Cook at a slow simmer for 3 to 4 minutes, until the whites are completely set and yolks are soft but no longer raw.

Divide the warm Moroccan sauce between six serving bowls (about 1 cup each). Top each with two poached eggs and sprinkle with panko and cilantro. Add a piece of garlic toast and serve.

Blueberry and Smoked Cheddar Beignets with Honey Ice Cream *Serves 6 to 8*

This showstopper of a dessert combines the sweet jammy flavor of blueberries with smoky sharp cheddar in light-as-air fritters. They're delicious with the accompanying fruit compote, lemony white chocolate crisps, and creamy honey ice cream, but they'd be just as wonderful dusted in powdered sugar and served up for brunch.

BLUEBERRY AND SMOKED CHEDDAR BEIGNETS In a small bowl, sprinkle the yeast over the warm water, add a pinch of the sugar, stir, and set aside until foamy. In a medium mixing bowl, whisk together the whole egg, egg yolk, and milk.

In the bowl of a stand mixer fitted with the dough hook attachment, mix together the remaining sugar, flour, mace, salt, and baking soda. Add the milk mixture, yeast, and melted butter. Mix on low speed for 4 minutes. Stop and scrape down the sides of the bowl with a rubber spatula. Mix on medium-low speed for 5 minutes to create a smooth, sticky, elastic batter. Scrape the bowl again, add the cheese, and mix for another 2 minutes. Remove bowl from mixer and gently fold in the blueberries by hand.

Cover the bowl with plastic wrap and let rest at room temperature for about 30 minutes, or, if not using right away, refrigerate it overnight.

BLUEBERRY AND SMOKED CHEDDAR BEIGNETS

1 ¼ tsp active dry yeast

2 Tbsp warm water (between 105°F and 110°F)

3 Tbsp granulated sugar (divided)

1 whole egg

1 egg yolk

⅔ cup whole milk

2 ½ cups all-purpose flour

⅛ tsp mace

¾ tsp salt

½ tsp baking soda

3 Tbsp unsalted butter, melted

½ cup shredded smoked cheddar, plus extra for garnish

1 cup blueberries

Canola oil, for frying

HONEY ICE CREAM

1 cup egg yolks (about 12)

2 cups heavy cream

1 cup whole milk

1 cup crème fraîche

⅔ cup granulated sugar

¾ cup honey

½ tsp salt

BLUEBERRY COMPOTE

2 cups blueberries

¼ cup sugar

1 ½ Tbsp light corn syrup

Juice of 1 lemon

⅛ tsp salt

2 Tbsp cornstarch

2 Tbsp water

continued overleaf

HONEY ICE CREAM Place the egg yolks in a medium mixing bowl. Wrap a damp kitchen towel around the base of the bowl (to keep it from moving when you whisk in the other ingredients).

In a medium saucepan, whisk together the cream, milk, crème fraîche, sugar, honey, and salt. Bring to just a simmer over medium heat, stirring frequently. Remove from heat and gradually whisk about a third of the hot cream mixture into the bowl of yolks (this tempers the eggs and keeps them from curdling). Pour the yolk mixture back into the pot and set over low heat. Whisking gently and continuously, cook until it reaches a temperature of 180°F and is thick enough to coat the back of a spoon. Remove from heat and pour through a fine-mesh strainer into a bowl. Set the bowl into a bigger bowl of ice water for about 30 minutes to quickly cool it down. Cover with plastic wrap and refrigerate overnight for the best flavor.

Churn the ice cream base in an ice cream maker according to the manufacturer's instructions until it's the texture of soft-serve. Transfer the ice cream to an airtight container and freeze for at least 12 hours to harden before serving.

BLUEBERRY COMPOTE In a small saucepan, combine the blueberries, sugar, corn syrup, lemon juice, and salt. Bring to a simmer over medium-low heat, stirring often. Cook until most of the blueberries soften and burst. Meanwhile, in a small bowl, whisk the cornstarch and water together. Add to the simmering blueberry mixture and cook for 1 minute, whisking the entire time, until thickened. Transfer compote to a bowl and chill. (It can be made several days ahead.)

continued overleaf

LEMON CRUNCH

1 ⅓ cups all-purpose flour

3 ¾ tsp cornstarch

¼ cup granulated sugar

⅛ tsp salt

½ cup (1 stick) unsalted
   butter, melted

¼ cup malted milk powder

Zest of 2 lemons

2 oz white chocolate,
   melted gently in a bowl
   set over barely simmering
   water or in a microwave
   at 50% power

SPICED SUGAR

2 cups granulated sugar

1 ½ tsp kosher salt

1 tsp ground cinnamon

⅛ tsp ground nutmeg

LEMON CRUNCH Preheat oven to 300°F. Line a rimmed baking sheet with parchment paper. In a mixing bowl, whisk together the flour, cornstarch, sugar, and salt until combined. Pour in the melted butter and mix with a rubber spatula until crumbly, breaking apart large clumps. Spread onto the baking sheet and bake for about 20 minutes, stirring halfway through, until crumbs are barely golden. Let cool to room temperature.

Transfer the crumbs to a mixing bowl and add the malted milk powder and lemon zest. Pour in the melted white chocolate and stir to coat the crumbs. Refrigerate the mixture, stirring every 5 minutes to break it into crumbs, until completely cooled. (It can be made several days ahead; store in an airtight container in the refrigerator.)

SPICED SUGAR In a large bowl, mix all the ingredients together until combined.

ASSEMBLY Preheat oven to 200°F. Set a cooling rack on a baking sheet and place in the oven to keep the cooked beignets warm. Line another baking sheet with paper towels or a clean, dry kitchen towel. Keep the bowl of spiced sugar nearby.

In a large saucepan or deep fryer, heat at least 2 inches of oil to 335°F (this can take 10 to 20 minutes). Working in batches, carefully lower tablespoon-size spoonfuls of batter into the hot oil and cook for about 4 minutes, turning often, until dark golden brown. Use a slotted spoon or tongs to transfer the beignets to the lined baking sheet and allow to drain. Place each hot beignet into the bowl of spiced sugar and toss to coat. Place on the baking sheet in the oven to keep warm while you cook the remaining beignets.

To serve, smear a large spoonful of blueberry compote on one side of each serving bowl. Pile the beignets on top of the compote. Place a handful of lemon crunch on the other side of the bowls, and sprinkle some more around the dish. Place a generous scoop of honey ice cream on top of the lemon crunch, and finish with a sprinkle of shredded cheddar.

Kachka

BONNIE MORALES
Kachka

YOU DON'T HAVE TO BE Russian to feel immediately at home, and even a little bit nostalgic, when you step through the doors at Kachka. There's something about the baroque wallpaper and vintage plates on the walls—echoes of chef-owner Bonnie Morales's childhood growing up as a first-generation Belarusian—that says "Grandma's house" no matter what your nationality. Yet despite this matronly aesthetic, three-year-old Kachka is not the least bit fusty; the cocktails are hip, the menu is cheeky, and somehow it always feels like a party.

It's no surprise, actually, considering Kachka is built on a foundation of vodka. The core of the restaurant's menu are little snacks called *zakuski,* things like smoked fishes and marinated mussels, made to be washed down with one of the eight dozen vodkas,

15 of which are housemade infusions like birch, tarragon, and horseradish (so popular it's available in retail by the bottle). When a menu is designed with imbibing in mind, things are bound to loosen up. Still, just as the old-country décor belies the party vibe, so too does the menu of Russian home cooking. Yes, Morales (née Frumkin) is recreating Soviet classics that grandmothers have been making for generations, but she's doing it with a precision and rigor befitting a chef who worked in such kitchens as the ultramodernist Moto in Chicago. And though her husband, Israel, runs the front of the house with the seemingly effortless grace of a dinner party host, he has the same haute pedigree, and it shows in the utter professionalism of his staff.

INGREDIENTS

2 oz Kachka horseradish vodka
  (see Note)

1 ½ oz fresh-pressed apple juice

Ice

¼ oz fresh-pressed beet juice

Triple Sunrise

Serves 1

Portland's favorite Russian hotspot proves not all brunch drinks must include tomato juice, Champagne, or egg whites. Two fresh juices, enlivened by spicy horseradish-infused vodka, provide the perfect wake-up call.

Note: If you can't get your hands on Kachka's horseradish vodka, you can infuse your own by adding a 3-inch piece of peeled fresh horseradish, cut into chunks, to a 750 ml bottle of vodka. Allow to steep for 3 days and up to 1 week before removing the horseradish.

METHOD Combine the vodka and apple juice in a cocktail shaker filled with ice. Shake vigorously until condensation forms on the outside. Strain into a double old fashioned glass filled with fresh ice. Drizzle beet juice on top.

2 ½ lb mussels, scrubbed and
   debearded
¼ cup low-sodium soy sauce
1 cup cold water
1 tsp granulated sugar
2 Tbsp white vinegar
4 Tbsp neutral vegetable oil,
   such as grapeseed (divided)

½ bunch fresh dill, finely chopped,
   plus extra sprigs for garnish
½ bunch fresh Italian parsley,
   finely chopped
Juice of ½ lemon
5 cloves garlic, smashed
1 ½ tsp kosher salt
½ tsp freshly ground black pepper
2 bay leaves
Sliced rye bread and salted butter,
   for serving

Crimean-Style Marinated Mussels *Serves 6*

These chilled marinated morsels are a common snack in the beachy resort city of Sevastopol on the Black Sea. This is just one of the many delicious little *zakuski* you might find on a Russian table — alongside vodka, of course.

METHOD Discard any mussels that do not shut when tapped or have broken shells. Refrigerate while preparing the marinade.

In a medium saucepan, combine the soy sauce, water, sugar, vinegar, 2 tablespoons of the oil, chopped dill, parsley, lemon juice, garlic, salt, pepper, and bay leaves. Bring to a boil over high heat. Reduce to a simmer and add the mussels. Cover and simmer for 7 minutes, until the mussels open.

Remove from heat and strain the mussels through a fine-mesh strainer set over a bowl. Discard any mussels that haven't opened. Refrigerate the cooking liquid. Remove mussels from shells. When liquid is cold, place mussels in liquid and refrigerate for at least 1 hour or until ready to serve. (The mussels can be prepared a day ahead and refrigerated.)

To serve, remove mussels from the marinade, arrange on serving plates or a platter, and dress with the remaining 2 tablespoons oil and dill sprigs. Serve with fresh rye bread and salted butter.

Langbaan

NOTHING CAN REALLY prepare you for a meal at Langbaan. There's not even a sign out front. Actually, that's not true. There is a sign, but it says PaaDee. That's because three-year-old Langbaan, which translates to "back of the house," is hidden (literally hidden—as in behind a fake bookcase) in the back of owner Earl Ninsom's more approachable Thai joint. Just pull the meat-grinder handle and cross the threshold into an entirely new take on Thai food.

Actually, that's not true either, because the ultracomplex Thai dishes prepared in this casual 24-seat space are actually quite old, born in 19th-century Thai palaces. They're new in that they've been modernized by 21st-century talents and are unlike anything else in Portland and, really, the country. You'll need to head to the award-winning Nahm in Bangkok, Langbaan co-chef Rassamee Ruaysuntia's old stomping grounds, to get anything even close. It's no wonder the James Beard Award semifinalist is booked up months in advance. Be persistent, though, and you'll be rewarded with a succession of about a dozen refined, intricate, and utterly surprising plates, including herbaceous salads and crystal-clear soups of startling complexity, from a menu that changes month to month, rotating through regions and principalities.

While you await your chance to experience this new-old side of Thai, you can visit the other stars in Ninsom's constellation, including PaaDee and year-old Hat Yai. Like Langbaan, they all blend a hip atmosphere with dishes that go far beyond the usual curries.

Pictured: Watermelon and Snakehead Fish Salad & Crispy Rice Cups with Galangal Cream

Watermelon and Snakehead Fish Salad (Tangmo Nar Plaa Hang)

Serves 6

The chefs at Langbaan strive to create balanced dishes, and this snacky salad — also known as *Tangmo Nar Plaa Hang* — hits all the flavor notes: hot, sour, salty, sweet, and umami. Although there's nothing technically challenging about this recipe, making it is an adventure. You'll need a vacuum sealer, access to a Thai grocery store, and the foresight to start preparations a day ahead.

Notes: Snakehead fish are a staple of Thai and Vietnamese cooking. Look for fillets that are brined and partially dried in the freezer section at Thai or Vietnamese grocery stores. | Tien ob, or scented Thai dessert candles, can also be found at well-stocked Asian markets and Thai grocery stores. They're traditionally used to perfume desserts, ingredients, or serving vessels with their smoke. In Portland, Chef Ninsom sources his at Lily Market, or you can buy them through online retailers like Amazon.com. | Pandan leaves can be found at Thai and Vietnamese markets. Fresh is preferable, but frozen is perfectly acceptable.

METHOD Heat the olive oil in a medium sauté pan over medium-high heat. Add the snakehead fish, skin side down, and cook for 5 minutes, until the skin is golden brown. Turn and cook the other side for another 5 minutes. Set aside to cool, then shred into small pieces. Return the sauté pan to low heat and add the shredded fish. Cook for another 10 minutes, stirring occasionally, until the shreds are golden brown.

Place the fish in a large glass jar or pot with a lid. Make room for a small bowl to nestle inside. Light a scented Thai dessert candle at both ends and set it in the bowl. Cover the jar or pot. Without oxygen, the candle will extinguish itself and release smoke. Refrigerate, covered, for 12 hours.

Cut the rind from the watermelon, making sure to leave about ¼ inch of flesh on it. Cut the green skin off the rind and discard. Cut the rind into 1-inch cubes and set aside.

INGREDIENTS

1 Tbsp extra-virgin olive oil

14 oz frozen snakehead fish, defrosted (see Note)

1 scented Thai dessert candle (see Note)

½ small seedless watermelon

¼ cup fresh coconut water

1 cup distilled white vinegar

½ cup granulated sugar

2 pandan leaves (see Note)

¼ cup canola oil, for frying

2 shallots, thinly sliced (divided)

1 Tbsp granulated sugar

1 Tbsp kosher salt

4 fresh kaffir lime leaves, sliced

¼ cup chopped fresh cilantro leaves, plus whole leaves, for garnish

2 baby zucchini, seeds removed, thinly sliced

1 Thai red chile, very thinly sliced, for garnish

Flaky sea salt, for finishing

Fresh mint leaves, for garnish

Cut the watermelon flesh into 1-inch triangles and be sure to remove all the seeds (even the white ones). In a vacuum-sealer bag, combine the watermelon flesh and the coconut water (use ¼ cup water per 25 to 30 triangles). Seal the bag with a vacuum sealer (it helps to hold the bag lower than the sealer to keep too much liquid from being pulled out). Refrigerate until ready to serve. (The watermelon is ready as soon as it's compressed, but it can be prepared and refrigerated up to several days in advance.)

In a medium saucepan set over low heat, combine the vinegar, sugar, and pandan leaves and cook for about 15 to 20 minutes. In a vacuum-sealer bag, combine the watermelon rind and vinegar mixture. Seal the bag with a vacuum sealer and refrigerate until ready to serve. (Again, it helps to hold the bag lower than the sealer to keep too much liquid from being pulled out. Refrigerate for 30 minutes or up to several days in advance.)

Heat the canola oil in a saucepan over medium heat. Fry half of the shallots for 10 minutes, or until browned and crispy. Use a slotted spoon to transfer them to a plate lined with paper towels and let drain.

In a medium bowl, combine the smoked fish flakes, fried shallots, sugar, salt, kaffir lime leaves, and cilantro.

Divide the compressed watermelon among the plates and top with the fish mixture. Divide the pickled watermelon rind, remaining sliced fresh shallots, and zucchini among the plates. Garnish with Thai chile slices, finishing salt, cilantro, and mint.

Crispy Rice Cups with Galangal Cream (Kanom Krok) Serves 8

These elegant little crispy cups hold the most luscious coconut cream with a little scallop salad on top. Also known as *Kanom Krok,* they've been blowing minds as one of the staple snacks served at Langbaan since it first opened. The restaurant uses a Japanese *takoyaki* pan, but you can also use an *aebleskiver* pan.

GALANGAL CREAM In a saucepan, combine the coconut milk, coconut water, galangal, lemongrass, lime leaves, rice flour, sugar, and salt. Bring to a simmer over medium-low heat and cook for 15 minutes. It will be very thick. (Only stir during the first 5 minutes, until the sugar is dissolved; any longer and the galangal will turn the cream a brown color.) Press the cream through a fine-mesh strainer to remove the herbs. The cream should taste salty, sweet, and creamy. Refrigerate until cold. (Cream can be made a day or two ahead and refrigerated.)

GALANGAL CREAM

1 cup coconut milk

1 ½ Tbsp fresh coconut water

1-inch piece fresh galangal, peeled and sliced

3-inch stalk lemongrass, sliced

4 fresh kaffir lime leaves, sliced

1 ½ Tbsp rice flour

¾ tsp granulated sugar

¾ tsp salt

CRISPY RICE CUPS

½ cup rice flour

1 Tbsp sticky or glutinous rice flour

1 cup coconut milk

SCALLOP CEVICHE

1 cup coconut milk

2 Tbsp grated palm sugar

3 Tbsp freshly squeezed lime juice

1 Tbsp fish sauce

6 dry-pack sea scallops, cut into quarters

1 stalk lemongrass, very thinly sliced

8 fresh kaffir lime leaves, very thinly sliced, plus extra for garnish

¼ cup chopped fresh cilantro leaves, plus extra whole leaves for garnish

CRISPY RICE CUPS Preheat oven to 325°F. Combine the rice flour and sticky rice flour in a mixing bowl. Slowly whisk in the coconut milk and strain the mixture through a fine-mesh strainer.

Preheat an oven-safe *takoyaki* or *aebleskiver* pan in the oven for 10 minutes. If it's not nonstick, brush each cup with vegetable oil. Pour 1 to 2 tablespoons of batter into each cup and tilt the pan to coat the sides evenly. Pour out the excess. Set the pan over low heat and cook the batter for 5 to 10 minutes, until it looks set. Transfer the pan back to the oven and cook for 20 to 30 minutes, until cups are golden brown. Remove from pan (if necessary, use the tip of a knife to separate the rice cups from the pan). Repeat with the remaining batter until you have at least 16 cups. (Rice cups can be made a day ahead. Store in an airtight container at room temperature.)

SCALLOP CEVICHE Combine the coconut milk, sugar, lime juice, and fish sauce in a mixing bowl and whisk until the sugar dissolves. Add the scallops, lemongrass, lime leaves, and cilantro. Refrigerate for 30 minutes.

TO SERVE If rice cups were made ahead, heat them in a preheated 325°F oven for 1 minute to recrisp. Fill each with 1 teaspoon of galangal cream. Top each with three pieces of scallop ceviche (use a fork to fish the pieces out of the liquid and let it drain off). Garnish each with a sprinkle of sliced kaffir lime leaves and a cilantro leaf.

Lardo

Lardo | Grassa

TECHNICALLY, Lardo is not named for the epithet you might want to hurl at yourself after eating the double burger with "porkstrami" and an entire plate of "dirty" fries topped with pork scraps and cheese (though it's easy to see how you might think so). This ridiculously good sandwich shop, which started as a cart and went brick-and-mortar in 2012, is named for an Italian delicacy of cured fatback — something humble that's been elevated, quite like what chef-owner Rick Gencarelli has done with sandwiches.

At Lardo, Gencarelli packs his sandwiches with the kinds of fine-tuned details normally reserved for upscale entrées. On one menu alone you can find pork given a Cuban mojo treatment, turned into Vietnamese-inspired meatballs, and roasted into a garlic-and-herb porchetta. And every month he invites another chef to collaborate on an epic special, with proceeds donated to charity. All that attention to detail makes sense given Gencarelli's fine-dining background, from Todd English's Olives to the Inn at Shelburne Farms. Still, even though the sandwiches — and the tap list — are serious, the rockin' vibe is anything but.

In 2013, he used the same recipe for success to launch fresh-pasta-focused Grassa. The modern, no-frills counter-service space belies some of the most complex pastas in town: squid ink chitarra with clams and preserved lemons, or the carbonara of your dreams with housemade bucatini and pork belly. Chef-driven dishes in a humble setting: it's the Gencarelli way.

1 cup rice wine vinegar

1 cup water

¼ cup granulated sugar

1 ½ tsp salt

2 large carrots, peeled and cut
into matchsticks (about 1 cup)

6-inch piece daikon radish,
peeled and cut into
matchsticks (about 1 cup)

½ cup mayonnaise

1 Tbsp Sriracha

1 Tbsp gochujang
(see Note)

1 ½ tsp rice wine vinegar

1 ¼ lb ground pork

2 scallions, sliced

1 ½ Tbsp Sriracha

1 ½ Tbsp fish sauce

1 egg, beaten

⅓ cup plus 1 Tbsp panko

1 tsp salt

1 Tbsp vegetable oil

4 ciabatta rolls, split

Fresh cilantro

Pork Meatball
Bánh Mì *Serves 4*

Other sandwiches on Lardo's menu may come
and go, but the meatball bánh mì is forever.
The trifecta of savory pork, pickled vegetables,
and spicy mayo makes it a hands-down
favorite. Each component can be made in
advance, which means you can bust one out
in short order any time the craving strikes.

*Note: Gochujang is a Korean condiment made with
red chiles, fermented soybeans, and sticky rice.
It has an earthy-spicy-sweet flavor profile. You
can find it at Asian markets or in the international
food aisle at some specialty supermarkets.*

PICKLED CARROT AND DAIKON RADISH
Combine the vinegar, water, sugar, and salt in
a saucepan set over medium-high heat. Bring
to a boil, stirring occasionally to dissolve
the sugar. Place the carrots and daikon in a
nonreactive bowl and pour in the vinegar
mixture. Allow to cool, then refrigerate for at
least 1 hour. (This can be made a week ahead.)

SRIRACHA MAYONNAISE Combine all the
ingredients in a small bowl and mix until
smooth. (The mayonnaise can be made a
week ahead and refrigerated.)

MEATBALLS Preheat oven to 375°F. Line a
rimmed baking sheet with parchment paper.

In a mixing bowl, combine all the
ingredients and use your hands to mix until
well combined. Roll the meat mixture into
eight 2-inch balls (about 2 ½ ounces each).
Place on the baking sheet and flatten slightly
with your palm. Bake for 12 minutes, rotate
the pan front to back, and cook for another
12 minutes, or until the internal temperature
of the meatballs reaches 160°F. Cut the
meatballs in half.

ASSEMBLY Preheat broiler. Heat the
vegetable oil in a nonstick sauté pan over
medium-high heat. Add the meatballs to the
pan and sear for 2 minutes, until crispy and
brown. Turn and sear for another 2 minutes.

Toast the rolls under the broiler, cut sides
up. Spread each with Sriracha mayonnaise.
Place a generous scoop of pickled carrot and
daikon radish on the bottom half of each roll.
Top with a generous pinch of fresh cilantro
and four meatball halves. Set the other half
of the roll on top, slice diagonally, and serve.

INGREDIENTS

Salt

1 lb bucatini

8 oz pancetta or guanciale,
   medium-diced

8 eggs (divided)

1 Tbsp coarsely ground black pepper

1 cup grated Pecorino Romano, plus
   more for garnish

1 cup grated Parmesan, plus more
   for garnish

2 Tbsp chopped fresh Italian parsley

Bucatini Carbonara with Sunny-Side-Up Eggs *Serves 4*

Carbonara has got to be one of the most soul-satisfying comfort-food dishes known to humankind. It's got it all: carbs, bacon, cheese — not to mention instant gratification, because it's ready in minutes. In this version from Grassa, chef Rick Gencarelli upgrades the classic with hearty bucatini, pancetta, two kinds of cheese, and an egg on top.

METHOD Bring a large pot of water to a boil over high heat and salt generously. Add the bucatini and cook until al dente according to package instructions.

Meanwhile, heat a small sauté pan over medium heat. Add the pancetta and sauté, stirring occasionally, for 5 minutes, until fat renders and the meat is deep golden and a little crispy. Use a slotted spoon to transfer the pork to a plate lined with paper towels. Reserve the pan with the pork fat to fry the eggs.

In a large bowl, whisk together four of the eggs, pepper, and both cheeses until well blended. Scoop out and reserve ½ cup of the pasta water, then drain the bucatini. Working quickly, add the bucatini and ¼ cup of reserved pasta water to the egg mixture in the bowl. Toss well for 1 to 2 minutes, until the cheese is melted and the sauce is creamy and starts to thicken and coat the noodles. If the sauce is too thick, add a bit more of the reserved pasta water to thin it out a bit. Toss in the crispy pancetta.

Set the pan of pork fat over medium heat. Add the remaining four eggs and cook until whites are set and yolks have thickened slightly. To help the whites cook, gently tip the pan toward you to pool some of the pork drippings, and spoon them onto the eggs until the whites are completely set. Then spoon a little on the yolks until they're done to your liking.

Divide the pasta between four bowls, top each with an egg, and garnish with parsley and a little more pepper, salt, and cheese if desired.

flour, scienc

Little T Baker

Little T Baker

DON'T WALK INTO Little T and expect cozy wood trim and pink boxes. This is not your grandma's bakery, not by a long shot. One look at the sleek, modern space and you know you're in the hands of someone who isn't afraid to spend some time on the cutting edge. When baker-owner Tim Healea opened the doors in 2008, he was part of a new era in modern American baking, one that drew inspiration not just from tweaking tradition, but, more importantly, from going back to the grain itself.

By experimenting with wheat varieties, alternative grains, and milling techniques, he developed some of the city's most sought-after breads—baguettes with a shatteringly crisp crust and an incomparably moist crumb; slabs of focaccia with both lightness and chew. And then he went deeper, offering a daily rotating cast of characters that showcase ancient grains and boundless creativity—boules of sourdough built on teff, or loaves of kamut and flint corn studded with raisins and rosemary. Of course, Healea knows we can't live by bread alone, which is why his kitchen cranks out a gorgeous array of sandwiches and his pastry case is filled with flaky chocolate praline croissants, delicate lemon curd tartlets, and the World Cup Pecan Puff, a creation of toasted pecan and vanilla frangipane that helped Healea and his teammates take the silver in the prestigious Coupe Du Monde de la Boulangerie baking competition back in 2002. Even his chocolate chip cookies venture far beyond the quotidian, but we've learned to expect nothing less.

Pictured: Chocolate Chunk and Roasted Hazelnut Cookies

Chocolate Chunk and Roasted Hazelnut Cookies *Makes about 30*

At Little T Baker, owner Tim Healea makes a point of using all Oregon ingredients for these super-chunky, crazy-delicious cookies, from the Camas Country whole wheat flour and Crémerie Classique butter to the bean-to-bar Woodblock Chocolate and roasted Freddy Guys Hazelnuts — both of which he adds with abandon. He keeps the nuts whole, allowing some to get broken up during mixing, but you can give them a rough chop if you wish.

Note: You can often find roasted hazelnuts in the bulk bin at well-stocked supermarkets. To roast your own, spread raw hazelnuts in an even layer on a rimmed baking sheet and toast at 350°F for 8 to 12 minutes, until beginning to darken and smell nutty. Transfer to a clean dish towel, gather the ends, and massage to remove most of the skins. Open carefully and separate the whole nuts from the dry skins.

METHOD Using a stand mixer or hand mixer, cream together the butter, sugar, salt, and vanilla on medium speed for 3 minutes, or until the mixture is fluffy and lightens in color. Stop to scrape down the sides of the bowl. On medium speed, beat in the eggs, one at a time, until incorporated.

In a separate bowl, sift together the pastry flour, whole wheat flour, baking powder, and baking soda. With the mixer on low, add the flour mixture in two additions. Stop and scrape down the sides of the bowl, and mix for another 30 seconds. Add the chocolate and hazelnuts and mix on low just until evenly distributed. Refrigerate the dough for several hours or up to 5 days. (For longer storage, portion the dough into balls and freeze on baking sheets until hard. Pack into ziptop freezer bags and store in the freezer for up to several months.)

1 cup (2 sticks) European-style
   butter, room temperature

2 ⅓ cups packed brown sugar

2 ½ tsp sea salt or kosher salt

1 Tbsp pure vanilla extract

2 eggs

2 cups pastry flour

2 cups whole wheat flour

2 ½ tsp baking powder

1 ½ tsp baking soda

11 oz bittersweet chocolate, chopped
   (about 2 cups)

2 cups roasted hazelnuts (see Note)

Preheat oven to 375°F. Line two rimmed baking sheets with parchment paper. Allow the dough to come to room temperature. Using a 2-ounce (#16) ice cream scoop, portion the dough into balls and set on the baking sheets, arranging them about 2 inches apart. Bake for 14 to 18 minutes, just until the edges are browned and cookies are barely set in the middle. Check the cookies halfway through. If they're baking unevenly, rotate the sheets from top to bottom and front to back. Allow cookies to cool on the baking sheets before transferring to a wire rack to finish cooling. Repeat with the remaining dough. Cookies will keep in an airtight container for several days.

POOLISH

3 cups artisan bread flour, such as
 Lehi Roller Mills artisan baking
 flour (or high-protein all-purpose
 flour, such as King Arthur brand)
Small pinch of instant or rapid rise
 yeast (about 1/16 tsp)
1 1/2 cups cool water (about 75°F)

DOUGH

4 1/2 cups artisan bread flour, such as
 Lehi Roller Mills artisan baking flour
 (or high-protein all-purpose flour,
 such as King Arthur brand)
1/2 tsp instant or rapid rise yeast
1 1/3 cups cool water (about 75°F)
1 Tbsp plus 2 tsp sea salt or kosher salt
Extra-virgin olive oil
2 cups pitted French green olives
 with herbs

Little T's Olive Slab

Makes 8 to 10 servings

Little T Baker's rich focaccia breads, or slabs, are renowned in Portland. It's nearly impossible to buy one for dinner and not snack on it all the way home. Baker-owner Tim Healea uses a pre-fermented dough to add flavor as well as lift. Start this dough the night before and you can have warm bread for dinner the next day. It also makes excellent sandwiches.

POOLISH Place flour in the bowl of a stand mixer. Dissolve the yeast into the water, then mix into the flour until fully incorporated. Cover the bowl with plastic wrap and allow to ferment for 8 to 12 hours at room temperature, until a few bubbles form on the surface.

DOUGH Add the flour to the bowl of poolish. Dissolve the yeast in the water and add to the bowl. Mix with a dough hook on low speed for 3 minutes, or until the ingredients are fully incorporated (the dough should be a little wet and sticky). Add the salt, increase speed to medium-low, and mix for about 5 minutes, until dough becomes smooth.

Transfer dough to a clean, lightly oiled bowl. Cover and let rise at warm room temperature (around 72°F) for 1 hour. Turn the dough out onto a lightly floured surface and fold it over onto itself two or three times (a bench scraper works best for this) to help increase its strength. Transfer the dough back to the bowl (no need to clean it), cover, and let the dough rise at warm room temperature for 1 hour. If your kitchen is cooler, allow the dough to rise a bit longer.

Brush a rimmed baking sheet (half-sheet size, or about 13 × 18 inches) with olive oil. Gently turn dough out onto the sheet pan. With a flat palm, pat out any big gas bubbles from the dough and stretch or press the dough until it almost reaches the edge of the pan (the thickness of the dough should come about halfway up the sides of the pan). Brush the top liberally with more olive oil. Allow the dough to rise in the pan for 45 minutes to 1 hour.

While the dough rises, preheat oven to 450°F. When the dough has almost doubled in size, press the olives randomly into the dough. Bake for 25 to 30 minutes, or until both the top and bottom of the slab are golden brown. With an offset spatula, remove the slab to a cooling rack and cool for at least 1 hour before cutting into squares and serving.

Mae

ONE OF THE BEST Southern meals in Portland is not at a restaurant. It's not at a cart, either. Or a pop-up. There's not much décor to speak of, and the beer and wine list is strictly BYOB. And, no, it's not at someone's house. It's a phenomenon called Mae, run by a young culinary powerhouse named Maya Lovelace, a North Carolina native who's basically breaking all the rules while opening our eyes to the deepest Appalachian culinary traditions.

Tucked in an event space behind Old Salt Marketplace, Mae "pops up" at the same time each week, except when it doesn't. To know if Monday's "meat and three," Wednesday's 10-course Southern bacchanalia, or Sunday's belly-busting brunch are on, you'll have to sign up for the mailing list. Instead of reservations, there are tickets, and when they go live you'll have to click fast because they sell out within minutes. Yes, the angel biscuits with pickled ramp pimento cheese and the bacon-fat-drenched mustard greens are that good. They're also served at communal tables, with everyone passing the dishes around family-style, so this is no place for the antisocial. But you wouldn't be here if you were, no matter how crispy, crackly, moist, and juicy Lovelace's fried chicken is, because Mae, at its heart, is a deeply personal experience. Every heaping platter Lovelace hands you comes with a story of heirloom recipes, ingredients, or growing up in the South. It soon becomes clear that Mae doesn't just share a name with Lovelace's grandma, it shares her spirit too.

1 lb dried elbow macaroni

¼ cup (½ stick) unsalted butter

¼ cup all-purpose flour

3 cups cold whole milk

1 cup cold heavy cream

1 tsp kosher salt

¼ tsp freshly ground black pepper

½ tsp granulated sugar

⅓ cup cream cheese, softened

4 cups shredded white cheddar

2 ½ Tbsp jarred pimentos

3 ½ Tbsp Crystal hot sauce, or to taste

½ tsp freshly squeezed lemon juice

1 cup crushed salt and vinegar potato chips (optional)

1 tsp smoked paprika (optional)

Sliced scallions or chives (optional)

Pimento Mac and Cheese *Serves 6*

The only thing better than rich pimento cheese is pimento cheese *with pasta.* At Mae, chef-owner Maya Lovelace stirs the Southern staple into her creamy mac and cheese and then takes the whole thing completely over the top with a sprinkle of crushed potato chips. She also adds a healthy dose of Crystal hot sauce, which has a tangy, flavorful heat that's not as searingly hot as some other brands. If you opt for a different sauce, proceed with caution.

METHOD Bring a large pot of water to a boil and salt generously. Add the macaroni and cook until just tender. Drain and set aside.

Melt the butter in a heavy saucepan set over medium-high heat. Stir in the flour and cook for 5 minutes. Whisk in the milk and cream, a little at a time, letting the roux absorb the liquid before adding more. Allow to simmer gently over medium heat for 2 to 3 minutes, until thick enough to coat the back of a spoon.

Add the salt, pepper, sugar, and cream cheese, stirring to combine. Stir in the macaroni, cheddar, pimentos, hot sauce to taste, and lemon juice. Continue heating gently over medium heat, stirring often to incorporate the ingredients and melt the cheese evenly into the sauce. Reduce heat to low, taste, and adjust seasonings if desired. (Once the cheese has melted, keep the heat fairly low or the cheese will separate and the sauce will become grainy.)

When ready to serve, ladle the pasta into bowls. Sprinkle with crushed chips, dust with some of the smoked paprika, and scatter scallions or chives over the top. (Pasta can be reheated in a saucepan set over medium heat. Add a small amount of milk and stir often until warmed through.)

CAKE

1 ½ cups (3 sticks) unsalted butter, room temperature, plus extra for greasing

1 cup granulated sugar

2 ½ cups dark brown sugar

5 eggs, room temperature

3 cups all-purpose flour

1 tsp salt

½ tsp baking powder

1 cup buttermilk, room temperature

1 tsp pure vanilla extract

1 tsp toasted pecan bitters, black walnut bitters, or pure vanilla extract

½ cup cocoa nibs, such as smoked nibs from Bourbon Barrel Foods, or toasted pecans

BROWN BUTTER ICING

½ cup (1 stick) unsalted butter

5 Tbsp whole milk

1 tsp pure vanilla extract

1 tsp toasted pecan bitters, black walnut bitters, or pure vanilla extract

2 cups sifted powdered sugar

½ tsp salt

Brown Sugar and Cocoa Nib Pound Cake with Brown Butter Icing Makes 1 (9 ½-inch) Bundt cake

Most dinners at Mae end with cake, in honor of chef Maya Lovelace's grandma, who used to sell her cakes to neighborhood restaurants to help make ends meet. Lovelace gives this golden beauty a nutty flavor with browned butter, pecan bitters, and cocoa nibs for bittersweet crunch. If you can't find cocoa nibs, she says it's just as delicious with pecans.

CAKE Preheat oven to 325°F. Generously grease a 9 ½-inch Bundt pan with butter.

Using a stand mixer or hand mixer, beat the butter on medium-high speed for 4 minutes, or until fluffy and lighter in color. Add both sugars and beat again for another 4 minutes, until light and fluffy. Scrape down the sides of the mixer bowl with a rubber spatula. With the mixer on medium speed, beat in the eggs one at a time, making sure each is incorporated before adding another.

Sift the flour, salt, and baking powder together into a medium bowl. Combine the buttermilk, vanilla, and bitters in a small measuring cup.

With the mixer on low, add the dry ingredients in three additions, alternating with the buttermilk mixture and making sure to allow each addition to fully incorporate before adding the next. Stir in the cocoa nibs.

Spoon the batter into the prepared pan and smooth the top. Bake on the center rack of the oven for 50 to 60 minutes, or until golden brown and a toothpick or knife inserted in the center comes out clean.

Set the cake on a wire rack to cool in the pan for 10 minutes. Invert the cake onto the rack, lift off the pan, and allow it to finish cooling to room temperature.

BROWN BUTTER ICING Melt the butter in a medium saucepan set over medium heat. Cook, whisking occasionally, until the milk solids have turned golden brown and smell nutty (be careful not to let the solids burn). Turn off the heat and immediately add the milk, vanilla, and bitters. The mixture will boil angrily for a moment, then settle down. Whisk in the powdered sugar and salt as quickly as possible, making sure to eliminate any lumps in the icing.

Spoon icing over the cooled cake and let it drip down the sides. Allow cake to stand at room temperature until glaze sets. Slice and serve.

KASEY MILLS

Mediterranean Exploration Company

DIFFERENT PEOPLE call it different things: Mediterranean Exploration Company, M.E.C., "That Gorham Place in the Pearl." But here's one thing everyone can agree on: this restaurant serves some of the finest Middle Eastern food in the city. It helps that it's co-owned by two veteran chefs who share not just the same vision, but commitment to detail, and who spent nearly a decade working side by side.

Kasey Mills, M.E.C.'s executive chef and co-owner, along with his mentor, John Gorham, spent seven years at Gorham's Toro Bravo before taking the leap to launch this slightly upscale joint in the summer of 2014. Their research trips to the Middle East paid off in richly spiced lamb cloaked in chewy pita, tender chicken with saffron yogurt and barberries, and silky hummus topped with a Yemenite chile-cilantro sauce called *s'hug*.

And it's all served up in a space as modern and fresh as their takes on Levantine cuisine itself, paired with one of the most exciting cocktail menus in the city.

Two years later, the team followed up on their success with Shalom Y'all, an Israeli street-food spin-off. With a focus on vibrant salads bursting with herbs and fresh pita sandwiches stuffed with smoky eggplant or grilled lamb, it brings M.E.C.'s rigor to the fast-casual set.

DRESSING

2 small lemons, cut in half

1 ½ tsp coriander seeds

1 clove garlic

½ tsp salt

1 tsp whole-grain mustard

1 tsp honey

½ cup extra-virgin olive oil,
   plus more for brushing

CANDIED PECANS

½ cup pecans, roughly chopped

3 Tbsp granulated sugar

SALAD

4 bulbs fennel, tops removed

6 stalks celery, ends trimmed

2 Tbsp fresh tarragon leaves

2 Tbsp finely chopped fresh chives,
   for garnish

1 Tbsp pistachio oil, for drizzling
   (optional)

Fennel Salad with Candied Pecans, Tarragon, and Grilled Lemon Vinaigrette *Serves 4*

Paper-thin slices of fennel and celery form the aromatic and crunchy-fresh base of this vibrant salad. Grilling the lemons before juicing concentrates their flavor and adds a delicious touch of smoke. If you don't plan to fire up the grill, sear the lemons in a hot pan instead.

DRESSING Preheat grill to medium-hot. Brush cut sides of lemons with olive oil. Grill the lemons, cut side down, until charred, about 3 to 4 minutes. (Alternatively, you can sear the lemons on a grill pan or sauté pan set over medium-high heat.) Transfer to a plate and set aside to cool. Squeeze the juice from the lemons and reserve. You should have about ¼ cup.

Using a mortar and pestle, pound the coriander seeds, garlic clove, and salt into a paste. Transfer the paste to a small mixing bowl and add the mustard, honey, and lemon juice. Slowly whisk in the olive oil in a thin, steady stream until emulsified.

CANDIED PECANS Preheat oven to 325°F. Using a colander, rinse pecans briefly with water, add the sugar, and then toss to coat. Arrange pecans in a single layer on a baking sheet. Bake for 10 to 15 minutes, until the nuts begin to brown. Set aside to cool. Use your hands to break up any nuts that are stuck together.

SALAD Use a vegetable peeler to remove the outer layer of the fennel and celery. Trim the root end of the fennel bulbs, cut in half lengthwise, and remove the cores. Use a mandoline to slice the fennel and celery very thinly. (Thin slices are the key to the salad.)

Mix the fennel, celery, candied pecans, and tarragon in a large bowl, and toss with ¼ cup of the dressing. Taste and add more dressing and salt and pepper if desired. Divide among plates and top with chives and pistachio oil, if using.

MARINATED CHICKEN

1 Tbsp coriander seeds
1 Tbsp cumin seeds
2 Tbsp grated fresh ginger
8 cloves garlic
1 Tbsp paprika
1 Tbsp curry powder
1 tsp chili flakes
Juice of 1 lemon

½ cup plus 1 Tbsp extra-virgin olive oil
   (divided)
2 Tbsp cold water
Salt and freshly ground black pepper
1 bunch fresh Italian parsley,
   roughly chopped
4 boneless, skin-on chicken breasts
1 Tbsp unsalted butter

SALAD

4 cups arugula
1 red onion, thinly sliced
¼ cup capers, chopped
Juice of 1 lemon
¼ cup extra-virgin olive oil
¼ cup grated Pecorino Romano
Salt and freshly ground black pepper

Moroccan Chicken with Arugula Salad Serves 4

Like all the dishes at Mediterranean Exploration Company, this one is layered with complex flavors at every step, from the evocative marinade with a bazaar's worth of spices, to the piquant salad of peppery arugula and Pecorino Romano. At M.E.C., chef Kasey Mills cooks the chicken under a brick, but says at home, pan-roasting is the way to go.

MARINATED CHICKEN Put the coriander and cumin seeds in a small skillet over medium heat and toast for about 3 minutes, until aromatic. Grind to a powder in a spice grinder or with a mortar and pestle. Transfer ground spices to a blender or food processor and add the ginger, garlic, paprika, curry powder, chili flakes, lemon juice, ½ cup of the olive oil, water, salt and pepper to taste, and parsley. Blend until completely smooth.

Combine the marinade and chicken breasts in a ziptop bag or covered baking dish. Allow to marinate in the refrigerator for at least 2 hours and up to 1 day.

When ready to proceed, preheat oven to 400°F. Heat butter and the remaining tablespoon of olive oil in a large oven-safe skillet over medium-high heat until the butter is melted and foamy. Add the chicken, skin side down, and reduce the heat to medium. Cook undisturbed for 5 minutes, or until the skin is golden brown and crispy and releases easily from the pan. Flip the chicken and cook for another minute, then put the pan in the oven. Bake for 8 to 10 minutes, depending on size, until cooked through and the internal temperature is 150°F. Transfer the chicken to a cutting board and let rest for 10 minutes. (The internal temperature will continue to rise a bit and the chicken will retain its juices.)

SALAD Toss the arugula, red onions, and capers together in a bowl. Add the lemon juice and olive oil and toss. Add the Pecorino Romano, toss again, and season with salt and pepper.

Divide the salad among four plates. Slice the chicken, set on top of the salads, and serve.

Milk Glass Mrkt

IT'S NOT OFTEN a little neighborhood café gets on *Bon Appétit*'s 50 Best New Restaurants list. And yet, of all the restaurants that opened in the nation, the little 28-seat Milk Glass Mrkt was so special it earned a spot in 2015. The thing is, if you know anything about chef-owner Nancye Benson, you know it's not all that surprising. This is a woman whose culinary talent and visual creativity are both cranked up to 11.

She originally earned her tastemaker rep with Moxie Rx, a pioneering food cart that was one of the first to serve restaurant-worthy food from a retro-cool trailer brimming with style, effectively setting the tone for a food-cart scene that inspired the nation. Her three-year-old Milk Glass Mrkt is like Moxie 2.0 — bigger, better, and, hallelujah, fully equipped with central heat. She shed the retro vibe in favor of a minimalist modern look. And in keeping with the name, she sells a slim collection of her favorite artisan goods. But the main draw here is her food. Benson's seasonally driven breakfasts, lunches, and sweets all straddle the line between totally approachable and delightfully surprising. She has a kale salad, yes, but it comes with a multitude of components, including savory granola and sweet dates tossed in garlic oil. These are the details that set Benson apart, and she's always been a stickler for them — even her cocktail list is far more developed than you'd expect from a counter-service café. But that's exactly why Milk Glass Mrkt is the little café that could.

Kale Salad with Pickled Onions,
Garlic Dates, and Savory Granola

SAVORY GRANOLA

2 ¼ cups rolled oats

½ cup sliced almonds

⅓ cup sunflower seeds

⅓ cup pepitas

3 Tbsp extra-virgin olive oil, plus extra for tossing

1 Tbsp plus 1 ½ tsp maple syrup

2 Tbsp poppy seeds

1 Tbsp flaxseed

½ tsp sea salt

½ tsp coarsely ground black pepper

2 cloves garlic, sliced paper-thin

SUNFLOWER DRESSING

½ cup plus 2 Tbsp extra-virgin olive oil

8 large cloves garlic

1 cup sunflower seeds

½ tsp kosher salt

⅓ cup packed fresh tarragon leaves

½ cup champagne vinegar

Zest of ½ lemon

Juice of 1 large lemon (¼ cup)

2 Tbsp honey

½ cup plus 2 Tbsp vegetable oil

¼ to ½ cup cold water

Kale Salad with Pickled Onions, Garlic Dates, and Savory Granola *Serves 8*

Nancye Benson's kale salad is legendary in Portland, and she says it's the one recipe her customers beg for the most. The secret is in how she layers it with so many flavors, from the crunchy granola to the pickled onions to the chewy dates tossed with garlic-steeped olive oil. There are lots of components, but they store well, making it easy to whip up another salad whenever the craving strikes.

SAVORY GRANOLA Preheat oven to 350°F. Mix the oats, almonds, sunflower seeds, and pepitas together in a medium mixing bowl. In a small bowl, combine olive oil, maple syrup, poppy seeds, flaxseed, salt, and pepper. Drizzle over the oat mixture and toss until evenly coated. Spread mixture on a rimmed baking sheet and bake for 15 to 20 minutes, or until the almonds are lightly golden.

In a small bowl, toss the garlic with a little oil to coat, then sprinkle over the granola. Toast in the oven for 10 minutes, just until the garlic is golden (be careful not to burn the garlic). Let cool, and store in an airtight container for up to 1 month.

SUNFLOWER DRESSING Combine the olive oil and garlic in a small saucepan over very low heat. Cook for 15 to 18 minutes, or until the garlic is tender and lightly browned. Allow to cool.

Combine the sunflower seeds and salt in a food processor and pulse until the seeds are very fine.

Strain the roasted garlic from the olive oil (reserving the oil). Add the garlic and tarragon to the food processor and pulse again until finely chopped.

Reserve 2 tablespoons of the garlic oil for the dates. With the machine running, add the rest of the garlic oil in a steady stream, and process until the mixture resembles nut butter, stopping to scrape down the sides of the bowl as necessary.

With the machine off, add the vinegar, lemon zest, lemon juice, and honey. Pulse to combine. With the machine on, gradually add the vegetable oil, but don't add the oil too slowly, as the dressing has a tendency to get too thick if overprocessed. Pulse in

GARLIC DATES

12 Medjool dates, pitted and
  roughly chopped
2 Tbsp garlic oil (see sunflower
  dressing method)

PICKLED RED ONIONS

¼ cup apple cider vinegar
¼ cup red wine vinegar
¼ cup water
2 Tbsp granulated sugar
1 Tbsp kosher salt
1 stick cinnamon
1 star anise
⅛ tsp red pepper flakes
1 red onion, sliced into ¼-inch-
  thick half-moons

ASSEMBLY

1 large delicata squash or 4 carrots
1 Tbsp extra-virgin olive oil
Salt and freshly ground black pepper
2 bunches Italian (lacinato) kale,
  stems removed and leaves torn
2 cups cooked lentils, garbanzo beans,
  or cannellini beans

¼ cup of the water to thin the dressing a bit. Taste and add more water if necessary. The dressing should be the consistency of a thick cream sauce and taste full-flavored with balanced acidity, not watery. (Dressing can be made a week ahead and refrigerated.)

GARLIC DATES Combine the dates and garlic oil in a small bowl. (Dates can be made several days ahead and refrigerated.)

PICKLED RED ONIONS Combine the apple cider vinegar, red wine vinegar, water, sugar, salt, cinnamon stick, star anise, and red pepper flakes in a medium saucepan. Bring to a simmer over medium heat. Cook for 2 minutes. Add the onions, reduce heat to low, and cook until the onions begin to give off some of their color. Remove from heat and let cool to room temperature. Refrigerate until cold before using. (Pickled onions can be made several days ahead and refrigerated.)

ASSEMBLY Preheat oven to 425°F. Cut the ends off the squash, cut in half lengthwise, and scoop out the seeds. Slice into ½-inch-thick half-moons (the skin is thin, tender, and edible, so there's no need to peel it). If using carrots, peel and cut into 2-inch chunks. Toss with olive oil, salt, and pepper. Set a rimmed baking sheet in the oven to preheat for 10 minutes. Add vegetables and roast until tender and beginning to brown, about 10 to 15 minutes for squash or 20 minutes for carrots.

In a large bowl, toss the kale with about 1 cup of the dressing, massaging the leaves a bit to soften them. Add half the strained pickled onions, garlic dates, 1 cup savory granola, half the roasted squash or carrots, and the lentils or beans. Toss with a little more dressing (about ½ cup) until ingredients are evenly coated to your liking. Transfer salad to a serving bowl and garnish with the remaining pickled onions and roasted vegetables and a sprinkle of savory granola.

FRUIT COMPOTE

1 lb firm fruit, such as apples or
  pears, peeled, cored, and cut into
  ½-inch pieces
⅓ cup granulated sugar, or to taste

¾ lb soft fruit, such as plums,
  apricots, figs, or berries, cut into
  ½-inch pieces if necessary
Spices, such as cinnamon, saffron,
  rose water, or star anise

BAKED OATMEAL

1 cup oats
5 eggs
3 egg yolks
1 tsp pure vanilla extract
1 tsp vanilla paste
⅓ cup granulated sugar
3 cups whole milk
1 cup heavy cream
Boiling water, for water bath

Baked Oatmeal Breakfast Custards with Fruit Compote *Serves 8*

These luscious, eggy custards straddle the line between breakfast and dessert, and they're perfect for serving a crowd at brunch. Toasting the oats first brings out their nutty flavor, which goes deliciously with seasonal fruit compote. Benson says just about any combination of firm and soft fruits, plus spices, will be delicious. Some of her favorite combinations include pear, fig, and star anise; apple, blueberry, and cinnamon; apple, plum, and rose water; and pear, apricot, and saffron.

FRUIT COMPOTE Heat apples or pears and sugar in a saucepan over medium heat until sugar melts and fruit begins to soften (add a little water or juice if the fruit seems dry). Add the soft fruit and spices to taste. Cook for 10 to 15 minutes, until fruits are tender but not completely turned to mush.

BAKED OATMEAL Preheat oven to 350°F. Bring a pot or kettle of water to a boil. Spread the oats on a rimmed baking sheet and bake for 5 minutes, or until lightly toasted. Keep the oven on.

Place eight 6-ounce ramekins into a baking dish or roasting pan. Add 2 tablespoons toasted oats to each ramekin. In a large bowl, whisk together the eggs, yolks, vanilla extract, vanilla paste, and sugar. Whisk in the milk and cream.

Divide the mixture between the ramekins. Pour enough of the boiling water into the baking dish to reach halfway up the sides of the ramekins. Cover roasting pan with foil. Bake for 15 minutes, rotate the baking dish front to back, and bake for another 10 minutes, until the custards are set. (At this point, check every 2 to 3 minutes. Some may set faster than others and should be removed from the oven.)

Transfer the custards to a rack to cool for a few minutes. Top with fruit compote and serve. (Custards can be made ahead and refrigerated before topping with compote. To reheat one or two custards, set in a steamer basket over a pot filled with a few inches of boiling water. Cover and steam over medium-high heat for about 8 to 10 minutes. To reheat more custards, set a cooling rack in a large sauté pan. Add water to the pan, set the ramekins on the rack, cover, and steam.

Eggs till 3pm Daily

tuesday
thru
saturday
9 - 4
am pm

sunday
9 - 3pm
am

Milk Glass Mrkt

LISA SCHROEDER
Mother's Bistro

THE MOTTO AT Mother's Bistro is "It's all about the love." And while the uninitiated might dismiss this as clever marketing, anyone who has dined at the chandelier-bedecked, curtain-draped downtown restaurant knows that it's not just a motto, but a mission. It's why there's "mac and cheese du jour." It's why the weekend brunch has drawn hordes for 17 years and counting. And it's why everyone feels welcome, from kids to celebrities. Indeed, Mother's is the go-to spot for presidents on the campaign trail (Bill Clinton), actors filming movies (Harrison Ford), and entertainers headlining at the Rose Garden (Robert Plant). That's a lot of love for a restaurant serving up "mom food."

But that's because chef-owner Lisa Schroeder takes her food very seriously. Trained in some of the finest kitchens in Manhattan (Lespinasse, Le Cirque), she uses French technique to layer every dish with flavor (what she calls giving it "love"), whether it's humble chicken and dumplings or something a little fancier like steak frites. Everything is made from scratch, from the stocks to the scones, because when your restaurant honors the most important job on the planet, you don't cut any corners.

INGREDIENTS

14 Tbsp (1 ¾ sticks) unsalted butter
  (divided)
2 ½ lb portobello, button, or cremini
  mushrooms, sliced (about 12 cups)
Salt and freshly ground black pepper
1 yellow onion, finely chopped
4 large shallots, finely chopped

½ cup dry sherry (not cooking sherry)
½ cup all-purpose flour
2 qt chicken stock or canned
  low-sodium chicken broth
1 ¼ cups heavy cream
2 tsp salt
1/2 tsp black pepper
Juice of ½ lemon (optional)
1 Tbsp chopped fresh Italian parsley,
  for garnish (optional)

Cream of Mushroom Soup *Serves 4 to 6*

Chef-owner Lisa Schroeder makes this flavor-rich and versatile soup with a mixture of portobello and button mushrooms, but says any combination of mushrooms — especially wild mushrooms — would be delicious. Just be sure to sear them properly, in small batches, to maximize their flavor. This soup freezes beautifully and can be used instead of canned in any recipe.

METHOD Melt 2 tablespoons butter in a large sauté pan over high heat, and add a third of the mushrooms to the pan. (You want just enough mushrooms to cover the bottom of the pan in a single layer; don't crowd the mushrooms or they will steam instead of sear.) Season the mushrooms with a pinch of salt and pepper, and cook, stirring occasionally, for 6 to 8 minutes, or until evenly cooked and golden brown. Transfer to a bowl and repeat with the remaining mushrooms, adding butter, salt, and pepper to each batch.

Melt 2 tablespoons butter in the same pan over medium-high heat, then add the onions and shallots. Sauté until they start to color around the edges. Lower heat to medium and sauté for another 10 to 12 minutes, until soft and translucent.

Return the sautéed mushrooms to the pan and add the sherry, stirring to scrape up any browned bits. Cook over medium heat until sherry is reduced by half. Remove from heat.

In a large saucepan, melt 6 tablespoons of the butter over medium heat. Whisk in the flour to make a roux and cook for 3 to 4 minutes, or until pale yellow and resembling fine, wet sand.

Whisk the chicken stock into the roux, a little at a time, allowing the roux to absorb the liquid before adding more. Bring to a boil over medium-high heat, lower to medium, and simmer for 10 minutes, stirring occasionally.

Stir in the mushroom mixture, bring to a boil over medium-high heat, lower to medium, and gently simmer, uncovered, for 15 minutes. Stir in the heavy cream and gently simmer for 15 more minutes, stirring occasionally.

Season soup with the 2 teaspoons salt and ½ teaspoon pepper. Taste and adjust seasoning as necessary. Add lemon juice if desired. Serve hot sprinkled with some chopped fresh parsley, if using. (If freezing this, or any other cream soup, let it completely thaw in the refrigerator before reheating. If you don't, the cream will break and look curdled.)

INGREDIENTS

2 Tbsp unsalted butter

2 large cloves garlic, finely chopped

2 ½ cups packed fresh spinach leaves

⅛ tsp freshly ground black pepper

½ cup sun-dried tomatoes packed
   in oil, drained and thinly sliced

¾ cup kalamata olives

16 eggs, beaten

1 ¾ cups crumbled feta

Greek Frittata

Serves 4 to 6

Mother's Bistro earned its place as one of the most popular brunch spots in Portland thanks to boldly flavored dishes like this frittata. Eggs and spinach form the backdrop, as briny kalamata olives go head-to-head with the intense flavors of sun-dried tomatoes and feta. As with most frittatas and omelets, this also makes a great scramble. If you decide to go that route, add the cheese at the end, just before you're about to turn off the heat. Serve this with roasted potatoes or a lightly dressed salad or simply garnished with extra spinach, sun-dried tomatoes, and kalamata olives.

METHOD Preheat oven to 450°F. Melt the butter in a 12- to 14-inch nonstick, oven-safe sauté pan (or use four 6-inch sauté pans for individual servings) over medium-high heat. Add the garlic and sauté until fragrant, about 1 minute. Add the spinach and pepper and sauté about 2 minutes, or until the spinach has wilted. Add the sun-dried tomatoes and olives, stir, and cook until warmed through.

Add the beaten eggs and cook, stirring occasionally, for about 3 minutes, or until the ingredients are evenly distributed and the eggs are halfway cooked but still very wet looking on top.

Remove from the heat and sprinkle the feta evenly over the top. Place the pan in the oven and bake for 7 to 9 minutes, until the eggs are puffy, the cheese has melted, and the frittata is cooked through.

Slide a rubber spatula between the pan and the bottom and sides of the frittata to loosen it. Set a large cutting board on top of the pan and invert. Lift the pan off, leaving the frittata on the board. Cut into eight wedges and plate one or two wedges per person, depending on appetite. Serve hot or at room temperature.

JORDAN FELIX & BEN GROSSMANN

Multnomah Whiskey Library

YOU CAN ADD Multnomah Whiskey Library's wall of whiskey to the list of Portland's most-photographed images. It's right up there with Old Town's White Stag sign and the view from Pittock Mansion. If you've seen it, you know why. It's a jaw-dropping sight — running the length of the wall and all the way up to the ceiling, the 1,500 bottles backlit and sparkling like treasure, with nattily dressed bartenders scurrying up and down the brass library ladders to fetch them.

But it's what's inside those bottles that counts, not to mention the experienced hands putting them to use. And to that end, you can add MWL to the list of Portland's game-changing bars. When it opened in 2013, the wood-paneled, leather-clad space not only boasted the best whiskey collection in the state, but also introduced a new style of cocktailing. Taking a page from restaurants, where guests always have a seat, MWL bartenders mix drinks tableside. With this emphasis on hospitality comes an important bonus: attentive staff who have the deep knowledge, and time, to help you explore new favorites.

To complement all those high-end spirits, chef Ben Grossmann uses the collection as inspiration, creating dishes like Bourbon-Molasses Glazed Chicken and Salt and Pepper Fries with Whiskey Sour Aioli. His menu of familiar yet refined plates is as closely curated as the spirits selection, but, like sipping an old fashioned on the leather couch by the fire, it's always just what you need.

Pictured: Bourbon-Molasses Glazed Chicken with Bitter Greens & Modern Cocktail

Bourbon-Molasses Glazed Chicken with Bitter Greens *Serves 4*

When you're the head chef at a place with one of the most impressive collections of whiskeys around, it's a no-brainer to use some of that liquid gold in your cooking. Multnomah Whiskey Library chef Ben Grossmann's super-easy finger-licking glaze combines the caramel undertones of bourbon with the burnt-sugar flavor of molasses. It's incredible lacquered on moist brined chicken, and would be just as delicious on pork chops or tenderloin. The sautéed bitter greens provide a delicious foil to the sweet glaze, and a touch of brown sugar keeps it all in harmony. Grossmann uses dandelion greens from Vibrant Valley Farm on Sauvie Island, but any bitter green works, including radicchio.

JUNIPER BRINE In a medium saucepan set over medium heat, combine water, sugar, salt, peppercorns, juniper berries, garlic, and rosemary. Heat until sugar and salt dissolve. Remove from heat and allow to cool completely. (Brine can be prepared a day ahead and refrigerated.)

Cut the chicken into serving pieces (freeze the back and wing tips for making stock, or discard). Place the chicken in a bowl or large ziptop bag. Pour in enough brine to cover. Seal or cover and refrigerate for at least 8 hours and up to 24 hours.

BOURBON-MOLASSES GLAZE Combine the bourbon, molasses, and vinegar in a small saucepan set over medium heat and whisk until well combined and bubbling. Remove from the heat and set aside.

JUNIPER BRINE

8 cups water

¼ cup packed brown sugar

½ cup kosher salt

1 Tbsp whole black peppercorns

1 Tbsp whole juniper berries,
    lightly crushed

2 cloves garlic, smashed

1 sprig rosemary

3 to 4 lb whole chicken

BOURBON-MOLASSES GLAZE

¼ cup bourbon

¼ cup blackstrap molasses

1 tsp cider or red wine vinegar

BITTER GREENS

1 Tbsp extra-virgin olive oil, plus
    more for chicken

1 Tbsp unsalted butter

1 large yellow onion, diced

1 tsp salt

2 bunches dandelion greens and
    stems, or 1 small head radicchio,
    roughly chopped (about 4 cups)

1 to 2 Tbsp packed brown sugar

½ tsp crushed red pepper flakes

BITTER GREENS Heat the oil and butter in a large sauté pan set over medium heat. Add the onions, season with salt, and sauté for 5 minutes, until soft and translucent.

Add the dandelion greens or radicchio, sugar, and red pepper flakes. Cook until the thickest pieces of the greens are tender and the juices evaporate. Remove from heat, taste, and season with more sugar or salt if desired. (The greens can be made several days ahead and refrigerated. Rewarm or bring to room temperature before serving.)

ASSEMBLY Preheat oven to 375°F. Set a cooling rack or roasting rack on a baking sheet. Remove the chicken from the brine and discard. Pat chicken dry with paper towels and set skin side up on the rack (no need to add salt, since the chicken has been brined). Brush with glaze. Roast the chicken in the top third of the oven for about 20 to 25 minutes, or until the internal temperature of the thigh is about 130°F to 140°F. Brush with glaze again.

Increase heat to 450°F and roast until the internal temperature of the thigh is 160°F (about 10 more minutes). If the skin isn't crispy yet, place under the broiler for a few minutes.

Divide chicken and bitter greens among plates. Drizzle with drippings from the baking sheet if desired (be judicious; they're delicious and flavorful, but a little salty). Serve alongside your favorite starch, such as grits or mashed potatoes.

Absinthe, for spritzing

1 1/2 oz Dewar's 12-year-old scotch

1/2 oz Banks 7 Golden Age rum

1 tsp lemon oleo saccharum
(see Note)

Dash of Regans' orange bitters

Lemon wheel and amarena cherry,
for garnish (optional)

Modern Cocktail

Serves 1

Hugo Ensslin's 1916 pre-Prohibition classic, the Modern Cocktail, gets an even more modern and refined spin at Multnomah Whiskey Library. The lemon oleo saccharum might sound intimidatingly geeky, but it's really just the syrup from sugar-steeped citrus peels. It adds an intense lemon flavor without the sharpness of juice. And the absinthe spritz is as easy as filling a little travel spray bottle, allowing you to add just a fragrant touch of the anise-flavored liquor to the drink.

Note: To make the lemon oleo saccharum, use a vegetable peeler to remove the peel from one lemon, leaving the white pith behind. Combine with ¼ cup granulated sugar in a glass jar or plastic container with a lid. Cover and shake until peels are well coated with sugar. Allow to sit for several hours, until the oils from the peels have mostly dissolved the sugar. Add 2 tablespoons hot water, stir to dissolve any remaining sugar, then strain out the peels. Refrigerate before using. (Mixture will keep refrigerated for several weeks.)

METHOD Place a large ice cube in a rocks glass. Spritz glass with absinthe. (Alternatively, you can chill the glass with smaller ice cubes, discard ice, add a small amount of absinthe, turn glass to coat the sides, discard the excess, then add the large ice cube.)

Combine the Dewar's, rum, and lemon oleo saccharum in a mixing glass with ice and stir with a bar spoon until chilled. Pour over the large ice cube and garnish with the lemon wheel and cherry, if using.

MULTNOMAH WHISK{E}Y LIBRARY

EST. 2013

1124 SW ALDER STREET
PORTLAND, MULTNOMAH COUNTY, OREGON 97205

Hours

MONDAY — THURSDAY FOUR O'CLOCK TO TWELVE
FRIDAY AND SATURDAY FOUR O'CLOCK TO ONE

Multnomah Whiskey Library

CATHY WHIMS
Nostrana

AT NOSTRANA, it's not unusual to spot families enjoying wood-fired pizza and beer while the next table is celebrating a special anniversary with a multicourse dinner complete with a $180 bottle of Barolo. That's what happens when a chef of Cathy Whims's talents decides to open an Italian-style "tavern"—it becomes everyone's go-to. A six-time James Beard Award finalist, her rustic Italian food is approachable to be sure—radiatore with ragu, wood-fired pork chops—but prepared with a level of expertise and precision you'd expect from a chef of her caliber.

At 12 years old, Nostrana is venerable by Portland standards, but never predictable. The hyperseasonal menu is apt to change several times a week, depending on which just-picked ingredients the farmers have brought in. Even so, it's fully grounded in the traditions of Italian cuisine. Whims has studied (and still does) with some of the most respected Italian chefs, frequently traveling to Italy and bringing back what she's learned and tasted—or even guest producers and chefs. From special dinners celebrating Italian feast days to multicourse dinners that take a deep-dive into a region, eating at Nostrana can be a delicious education. The drinks menu is no different. The wine list is heavy with Italian varietals from all regions, and the renowned bar, backed by a seriously knowledgeable crew, produces cocktails that make creative use of Italian amari. If you've ever wanted to explore the vast world of bitter herbal liqueurs, Nostrana is happy to oblige.

Pictured: Quintessential Negroni

INGREDIENTS
1 oz Campari
1 oz Bombay dry gin
1 oz Cinzano sweet vermouth
Ice
Orange peel, for garnish

Quintessential Negroni *Serves 1*

In many ways, Portland has Nostrana to thank for putting this classic Italian cocktail on its radar and inspiring a week-long celebration. That's because for years they've been toasting to the drink's versatility with a "Negroni of the Month" program and have even invited bartenders from around the country to showcase their recipes. The program sparked a coveted industry party called the Negroni Social, which then brought national magazine coverage, and soon national Negroni Week was born. Herewith is the drink that started it all.

METHOD Stir all the ingredients in a mixing glass with ice until chilled. Strain into a rocks glass with large ice cubes or in a chilled coupe. Garnish with orange peel and serve.

INGREDIENTS

4 Tbsp (½ stick) unsalted butter (divided), plus more for greasing

¼ cup dry breadcrumbs or panko

3 stalks cardoon (see Note)

Juice of 1 lemon

½ small onion, finely chopped

Salt and freshly ground black pepper

2 Tbsp all-purpose flour

1 cup whole milk

2 eggs, separated

¼ cup grated Parmesan, plus extra for garnish

Cardoon Sformati

Serves 4

These delicious Italian custards are wonderful as a side dish to roasted meats, but they are just as delicious alongside a lightly dressed salad for brunch or lunch. Cardoons look a lot like giant celery, but they're related to artichokes and have a similar flavor. You can find them at farmers' markets from late fall through spring.

Note: When cardoons are out of season, you can use frozen artichoke hearts. Defrost 1 cup (about 6 oz) frozen artichoke hearts and roughly chop. Sauté along with the onions.

METHOD Preheat oven to 350°F. Butter four 6-ounce ramekins and coat with the breadcrumbs, tapping out the excess. Bring a pot or kettle of water to a boil.

Trim the ends of the cardoons and use a vegetable peeler to remove the outer strings. Cut into ½-inch squares and place in a bowl of cold water mixed with the lemon juice; let sit for 30 minutes (this will lessen any bitter aftertaste). Bring a pot of water to a boil over high heat and salt generously. Add the cardoons and boil for 15 to 20 minutes, until tender. Drain.

Melt 2 tablespoons of butter in a medium sauté pan over medium-low heat. Add the cardoons and onions and season with salt and pepper to taste. Gently cook for about

15 minutes, until the onions are golden and the cardoons are meltingly soft. Set aside to cool to room temperature.

To make the béchamel, melt the remaining 2 tablespoons of butter in the sauté pan over medium heat. Stir in the flour and cook for 5 minutes. Whisk in the milk, a little at a time, letting the roux absorb the liquid before adding more. Allow to simmer gently over medium heat for 2 to 3 minutes, until thick enough to coat the back of a spoon. Season with salt and pepper. Allow to cool. In a large bowl, combine the egg yolks, cardoon and onion mixture, béchamel, Parmesan, and salt and pepper to taste.

In the bowl of a stand mixer fitted with the whisk attachment, whip the egg whites until they form soft peaks (alternatively, you can do this by hand with a whisk). Fold the egg whites into the custard.

Divide the mixture among the prepared ramekins. Set in a roasting pan and add enough of the hot water to go halfway up the sides of the cups. Bake, uncovered, for 30 to 40 minutes, or until puffed, golden brown, and set. Remove the cups from the hot water bath.

To unmold, run a paring knife around the edge of the custards and tip them out onto plates. Garnish with grated Parmesan and serve.

ALEX GANUM, BEN MEYER, & MARCUS HOOVER

Old Salt Marketplace | Grain & Gristle

LOCAL, SUSTAINABLE, seasonal, farm-to-table. These buzzwords have been bandied about for so long and with such frequency, they've started to lose their meaning. But at Old Salt Marketplace, they're not just words, they're its raison d'être. No restaurant in Portland walks the talk better, and no other restaurant is as committed to teaching its customers to do the same at home. Consider this: half the space is devoted to a separate deli/butcher shop, selling meats broken down from whole, locally raised animals and then aged, smoked, or sausaged for good measure. In the Carver Room out back (also home to Mae, page 114), chef-owner-butcher Ben Meyer teaches an ongoing series of classes, from the basics (winter-meat cookery) to the ambitious (how to cure your own pancetta). As for the supperhouse itself, co-owner/designer

Marcus Hoover decked it out in wood from old barns and artwork by local artists, a backdrop befitting the rustic-chic menu of dishes like hearth-roasted beef with romesco.

While Old Salt opened in 2013, its beer-driven brother, Grain & Gristle, got a couple years' head start. It's cut from the same cloth, but here the vibe is more brewpub, without the bro factor. This is where the third owner, brewer Alex Ganum of Upright Brewing, really gets to shine. He's curated a tap list of first-rate craft beers, including the French and Belgian farmhouse ales he's known for, and G & G's simple, rustic plates, like roast pork with succotash or mussels and frites, are designed to go with them.

Char-Grilled Beef Bavette with
Chimichurri and Citrus Aioli

Char-Grilled Beef Bavette with Chimichurri and Citrus Aioli *Serves 8*

Bavette is the French (and much more appealing) term for flap meat, which is a thin and full-flavored beef steak from the belly area. It's a best seller at Old Salt Marketplace, both in the meat case and the restaurant, where it's char-grilled and served with bold sauces like this chimichurri and citrus aioli. Seek it out from a good butcher before it gets too popular and pricey.

BAVETTE Generously salt the bavette on all sides and set aside for 1 hour at room temperature.

CHIMICHURRI Meanwhile, in a medium bowl, combine the vinegar, salt, garlic, shallot, and chile. Let stand for 20 minutes. In a separate bowl, combine the cilantro, parsley, oregano, and oil. (Keep separate until just before serving to keep herbs vibrant.)

BAVETTE

¼ cup kosher salt

3 lb beef bavette steak

CHIMICHURRI

½ cup red wine vinegar

1 tsp kosher salt

4 cloves garlic, finely chopped

1 shallot, finely chopped

1 Fresno chile pepper or red jalapeño pepper, finely chopped

½ cup finely chopped fresh cilantro

¼ cup finely chopped fresh Italian parsley leaves

2 Tbsp finely chopped fresh oregano leaves

¾ cup extra-virgin olive oil

CITRUS AIOLI

2 cloves garlic

2 cups extra-virgin olive oil (divided)

2 egg yolks

Zest and juice of 1 lemon

Zest and juice of 2 limes

½ tsp kosher salt

CITRUS AIOLI In a food processor, process the garlic with just enough oil to make a paste, scraping the sides to make sure all of the garlic gets processed. Add the yolks and process until color lightens and mixture thickens. With the motor running, very slowly drizzle in the remaining oil in a thin, steady stream, allowing the oil to fully incorporate as you go. If the aioli gets too thick, add a splash of cold water and mix until it fully incorporates. Add the zest and juice of the lemon and limes, season with salt, and process until fully combined. Refrigerate for 30 minutes.

ASSEMBLY Build a very hot bed of coals in a charcoal grill (don't skimp on coals!). Brush off any excess salt from the meat. Set the meat as close to the coals as possible and grill for about 5 minutes per side (you're aiming for a thick char). Remove from heat and allow the steak to rest for at least 8 minutes before slicing it thinly across the grain.

Meanwhile, mix the two bowls of the chimichurri ingredients together. Arrange the steak on a serving platter, spoon the chimichurri on top, and serve the aioli on the side for dipping.

Toasted Wheat Berry Salad with Roasted Squash, Pickled Currants, and Hazelnuts *Serves 4 to 6*

Toasting wheat berries before cooking accentuates their flavor, bringing out a nuttiness that goes deliciously with the toasted hazelnuts and roasted squash. The pickled currants add a lively brightness. Try adding them to other salads, too, or even serving them with roasted pork.

METHOD Combine the vinegar, honey, cloves, and cinnamon in a medium saucepan and bring to a gentle boil over medium heat. Simmer for 20 minutes.

Place the currants in a nonreactive mixing bowl. Strain the liquid over the currants, stir, and set aside to cool to room temperature. Transfer to a mason jar and refrigerate until ready to use. (Currants can be made ahead and refrigerated for several weeks.)

Preheat oven to 350°F. Spread the wheat berries evenly on a rimmed baking sheet and toast in the oven for 5 to 10 minutes, stirring occasionally, until they smell nutty and darken slightly. Remove from heat but keep the oven on. Meanwhile, bring a large pot of water to a boil over high heat and salt generously.

Allow the wheat berries to cool for several minutes before adding them to the boiling water. Reduce to a simmer and cook, stirring occasionally, for 30 to 40 minutes until the berries burst but aren't mushy.

INGREDIENTS

1 cup red wine vinegar

½ cup honey

3 whole cloves

1 stick cinnamon

1 cup dried currants

1 cup wheat berries

1 cup hazelnuts

1 medium delicata squash

1 Tbsp plus ¼ cup extra-virgin olive oil
  (divided)

Salt

1 bunch fresh Italian parsley, leaves
  picked and chopped

3 sprigs winter savory or thyme,
  leaves picked and roughly chopped

Drain, cool, and refrigerate until ready to use. (Wheat berries can be prepared up to a week ahead.)

While wheat berries cook, spread the hazelnuts in an even layer on a rimmed baking sheet and toast in the oven for 8 to 12 minutes, until they look toasted and smell nutty. Remove from the oven and set aside. When cool enough to handle, spread the nuts on a large kitchen towel, gather the ends, and massage to remove most of the skins. Open carefully and separate the whole nuts from the dry skins. Use a heavy knife to roughly chop the nuts, leaving plenty of large pieces.

Increase oven temperature to 425°F. Slice the ends off the squash, cut in half lengthwise, and scoop out the seeds. Slice into ½-inch-thick half-moons (the skin is thin, tender, and edible, so there's no need to peel it). In a mixing bowl, toss the squash with 1 tablespoon of the olive oil, salt generously, and spread evenly on a rimmed baking sheet.

Roast for 10 to 15 minutes, until tender and beginning to brown. (Don't overcook or the squash will be mushy.)

In a large bowl, combine the cooked and cooled wheat berries, roasted squash (you can cut it into smaller pieces if you prefer), chopped hazelnuts, parsley, and chopped savory. Strain the currants, reserving the brine. Add the currants to the bowl and enough of the brine to dress the salad. Finish with the remaining ¼ cup olive oil. Taste and adjust the seasoning or add more oil if necessary. Serve at room temperature. The salad will keep, refrigerated, for 2 to 3 days.

Old Salt Marketplace

Olympia Provisions

CONSIDERING THE sheer volume of award-winning charcuterie produced in Olympia Provisions' meat-curing facility, it would be easy for the company's two restaurants to get lost in its shadow. The fact that they don't, that they're perennially at the top of everyone's must-eat list, is proof of the talent fueling them. It's a dream team, really. Among the key players are veteran chefs Alex Yoder and Eric Joppie leading the kitchens with big flavors, and "celebrity salumist" Elias Cairo providing the artisan meats and national cred.

OP first set up shop in the industrial eastside's Olympic Mills building in 2009, with a teeny, 900-square-foot curing facility and attached restaurant aimed at the nearby office workers. But word quickly spread, crowds and accolades flooded in, and two years later a second location was born—with a much bigger meat plant and walls of windows flooding the space with light. Of course, the meat shop outgrew its digs again (it now has 34,000 square feet all to itself), but the restaurants are staying put, offering dishes grounded in Northwest ingredients yet marching to a distinctly Mediterranean beat—think prime rib with bitter greens, or halibut with spicy Andouille sausage, made in-house, of course. Though the meat operation and the restaurants could certainly survive without each other, they're both that much better for the partnership. The chefs have the full lineup of OP's award-winning products at their fingertips, and we have two places bringing them to life.

8 oz unsliced ham (such as Olympia
 Provisions' sweetheart ham)

1 yellow onion, cut into large chunks

1 carrot, cut into large chunks

1 stalk celery, cut into large chunks

8 extra-large shrimp (26/30 count),
 peeled and deveined, shells
 reserved

Kosher salt and freshly ground
 black pepper

1 lb Manila clams, rinsed

2 (4 to 5 oz) Andouille sausages
 (such as Olympia Provisions),
 cut into ½-inch-thick rounds
 on a slight diagonal

1 ear yellow corn, cut into
 8 (1-inch) rounds

4 (5 oz) halibut fillets, about
 2 inches thick, skin removed

Canola oil

2 scallions, white and green parts,
 thinly sliced diagonally

⅓ cup thinly sliced fresh basil leaves

Lemon juice, to taste

Pan-Roasted Halibut with Shrimp, Clam, and Andouille Stew *Serves 4*

Mild-mannered halibut is the perfect foil for a rich stew made with ham broth, shellfish, corn, and spicy sausages.

METHOD Preheat oven to 350°F. Cut the ham in half. Combine with the onions, carrots, celery, reserved shrimp shells, and 4 cups of water in an 8-inch square baking dish. Cover with foil and bake for 3 hours. Strain and reserve the broth — you should have 2 cups. (If the broth has reduced to less than 2 cups, top off with water.) Discard the solids except for the ham. When cool enough to handle, shred the ham and reserve. (The broth and ham can be made several days ahead and refrigerated.)

Season the shrimp lightly with salt and pepper. In a large sauté pan, preferably with high sides, combine the broth, clams, shrimp, sausage, and corn. Cover and set over medium-high heat. Cook, stirring occasionally, for about 6 minutes, until the clams open and the shrimp are fully cooked. Set aside (remove and discard any clams that haven't opened).

Preheat oven to 350°F. Season the halibut fillets with salt and pepper. In a separate oven-safe sauté pan (large enough to hold the fillets without touching) set over medium-high heat, heat enough canola oil to cover the bottom of the pan. When the oil begins to smoke, add the fillets, and cook over medium heat for 5 minutes, or until a golden crust begins to develop. Transfer the pan to the oven and cook for another 2 minutes. Flip the fillets and bake for another 3 minutes, or until a metal skewer slides in and out without resistance. Set aside.

Return the pan with the shellfish stew to medium heat and add the reserved shredded ham, scallions, and basil. Bring to a simmer and season to taste with salt, pepper, and lemon juice.

To serve, divide the shellfish stew between four serving bowls. Top each with a halibut fillet and season with additional lemon juice, if desired.

BREAD PUDDING

1 ¼ cups heavy cream

3 eggs

Kosher salt and freshly ground
  black pepper

6 (1-inch-thick) slices day-old
  artisan bread, cut into cubes
  (about 6 cups)

Unsalted butter, for greasing

1 cup shredded aged white cheddar

¼ cup grated Grana Padano

Savory White Cheddar Bread Pudding with Mushroom Ragout and Fried Eggs *Serves 4*

Chef Alex Yoder admits his popular brunch dish has a lot of components, "but it's worth it," he says. "It's big on flavor." Best of all, each one can be made in advance, making day-of preparations a snap.

BREAD PUDDING Combine the cream and eggs in a medium bowl and whisk until fully combined. Season with salt and pepper to taste. (It will need to be a bit saltier than you want the finished bread pudding to be.) Add the cubed bread and stir to combine. Cover bowl with plastic wrap and refrigerate overnight.

Preheat oven to 350°F. Butter an 8-inch square baking dish and line it with foil. Coat the foil in butter. Fold both cheeses into the bread pudding until evenly combined. Pack the bread pudding tightly into the baking dish, making sure there are no pockets of air. Bake on the center rack of the oven for 30 minutes, or until set and a metal skewer inserted into the center is hot to the touch.

Allow to cool to room temperature, then refrigerate for at least 3 hours or overnight. Remove the bread pudding from the baking dish. Peel off the foil and cut in half lengthwise and crosswise into four uniform squares. Trim off and discard the edges.

MUSHROOM STOCK Combine all the ingredients in a small pot and bring to a boil over high heat. Reduce to medium-low and simmer for 45 minutes, or until the liquid is reduced to 2 cups. Strain into a bowl and discard the solids. (Stock can be made several days ahead and refrigerated.)

MUSHROOM STOCK

2 cups loosely packed dried
  porcini mushrooms

1 yellow onion, chopped

1 carrot, cut into 1-inch lengths

1 stalk celery, cut into 1-inch
  lengths

1 bay leaf

5 cups water

MUSHROOM RAGOUT

3 cups wild mushrooms, torn into
  bite-size pieces

Olive oil, for roasting

Kosher salt and freshly ground
  black pepper

5 Tbsp (½ stick plus 1 Tbsp)
  unsalted butter

5 cups sliced cremini mushrooms

1 yellow onion, finely chopped

1 ¼ tsp tomato paste

1 cup Marsala wine

ASSEMBLY

½ cup heavy cream

Kosher salt and freshly ground
  black pepper

2 Tbsp unsalted butter

Canola oil, for frying

8 eggs

2 scallions, thinly sliced diagonally

MUSHROOM RAGOUT Preheat oven to 350°F. In a large bowl, combine the wild mushrooms with just enough olive oil to coat, and sprinkle with salt and pepper to taste. Spread out on a baking sheet and roast for 10 minutes, until browned.

Melt the butter in a medium sauté pan over medium heat, then add the cremini mushrooms. Season with salt and cook, stirring frequently, until the liquid released by the mushrooms evaporates and the mushrooms are nicely browned.

Add the onions and cook over medium-low heat for 5 minutes. Add the tomato paste and cook for another 3 minutes. Add the Marsala and cook, stirring frequently, until it has reduced to a syrup. Add the mushroom stock and roasted wild mushrooms, stir, and remove from the heat. (Ragout can be made several days ahead and refrigerated.)

ASSEMBLY Combine the mushroom ragout and heavy cream in a large sauté pan. Bring to a boil and cook until the liquid is thickened but still pourable, about 10 minutes. Season with salt and pepper to taste, and keep warm.

Heat the butter in a large nonstick sauté pan over medium heat, then add the slices of bread pudding, cut side down, and cook until nicely browned. Repeat on the other cut sides. Blot the slices dry on paper towels, then transfer them to four warm plates. Top each with the mushroom ragout.

Add enough canola oil to the sauté pan to generously cover the bottom and set over medium heat. Add the eggs (if necessary, use two pans or work in batches) and cook, spooning hot oil over the whites, until whites are set. Spoon some of the hot oil over the yolks a few times until done to your liking. Season with salt and pepper to taste, and divide evenly between the four plates. Sprinkle each plate with the sliced scallions and serve.

SCOTT DOLICH & DAVID SAPP

Park Kitchen

IT'S IMPOSSIBLE TO imagine Portland's restaurant scene without Park Kitchen. For 14 years, this sliver of a spot overlooking the North Park Blocks has been a proving ground for some of the most talented chefs, bartenders, and food producers in the city. Like ripples in a pond, they've gone on to spread their own influence across town. But they can all trace their lineage back to Park Kitchen and to owner Scott Dolich, who seems to thrive on giving his staff creative license to make their marks on the menu. His reward is ours as well—a restaurant that serves up some of the most inspired plates in the city. Grab a seat at the bar or breezy sidewalk table and let chef David Sapp surprise you with plates that pull inspiration from anywhere and everywhere, but don't be surprised that they work. With dishes like Oregon albacore with Spanish Padrón peppers and French aioli spiked with Korean *gochugaru,* he's proving that when it comes to cooking, there are no boundaries.

Dolich's own pedigree is itself a litany of restaurants that broke the city's dining scene wide open: Zefiro, Pazzo, Wildwood, and Higgins. They each made indelible marks on the landscape, shaping our tastes and raising our expectations. That Dolich honed his skills in these kitchens speaks volumes, and he's using Park Kitchen to pay it forward.

Pictured: Cauliflower Ravioli with Laurel Broth, Pickled Sultanas, and Charred Cipollini Onions

Cauliflower Ravioli with Laurel Broth, Pickled Sultanas, and Charred Cipollini Onions

Serves 4

If you're looking for a special-occasion dish that can be made ahead of time, look no further. The delicate ravioli filled with silky cauliflower purée freeze beautifully, as does the broth, and the pickled golden raisins will keep for a week. Chef David Sapp says he developed the recipe to use up leftover cauliflower stalks, making these luscious bites the most genius use of compost fodder ever. Technically, the recipe makes double the ravioli you'll need for four servings. Just freeze the rest and another exquisite dinner is that much closer.

CAULIFLOWER RAVIOLI Melt the butter in a large saucepan set over medium heat. Add the cauliflower, onions, and salt. Cover and cook for 10 minutes, until the vegetables are soft but not browned. Add the garlic and cream. Cook, uncovered and stirring regularly, until the cauliflower has completely broken down and the mixture has thickened, about 5 minutes more. (Be careful not to scorch the bottom of the pan.)

Put the mixture in a blender or food processor and purée, with the lid ajar to allow the steam to escape, until smooth.

(Work in batches if necessary.) Add the cheese and gelatin and blend until extremely smooth.

Pass the mixture through a fine-mesh strainer set over a bowl to catch any large pieces that didn't blend, and set aside to cool. Spoon into a piping bag or ziptop bag, pressing out any air. Refrigerate until ready to use. (Filling can be made several days ahead and refrigerated.)

In a small bowl, beat the egg well. If using a ziptop bag, cut off one corner. Set a parchment-lined baking sheet nearby.

Place two wonton wrappers on a clean work surface. In the center of one wonton wrapper, pipe 1 tablespoon of cauliflower filling. Using a pastry brush, gently brush the beaten egg along the edges of the wrapper around the cauliflower filling. Place the other wonton wrapper on top and gently press down around the filling to remove any air pockets and secure the wrappers together. Using a fluted circular cutter or pasta wheel, cut around the filling, leaving a ¼-inch area of sealed dough. Place on the lined baking sheet and repeat with the remaining filling and wonton wrappers. Freeze until firm. (Ravioli can be sealed in ziptop bags and frozen for several months.)

CAULIFLOWER RAVIOLI

1 Tbsp unsalted butter

2 ½ cups roughly chopped cauliflower (florets and/or stalks, from about ½ large head)

1 large onion, chopped

2 tsp salt

2 cloves garlic, finely chopped

1 cup heavy cream

¼ cup grated Grana Padano

1 tsp powdered gelatin

1 egg

2 (12 oz) packages square wonton wrappers

LAUREL BROTH

2 tsp canola oil

1 large onion, sliced

2 bay leaves

2 cloves garlic, smashed

3 cups water

Salt

PICKLED SULTANAS

¼ cup sultanas (golden raisins)

¼ cup sherry vinegar

½ cup water

1 Tbsp granulated sugar

¼ tsp salt

CHARRED ONIONS

8 small cipollini onions, peeled and cut in half from top to bottom

1 tsp canola oil

¼ tsp salt

¼ cup dry sherry

½ cup cold water

ASSEMBLY

Toasted walnuts, for garnish

Peppery olive oil

LAUREL BROTH Heat oil in a large sauté pan over medium-low heat. Add the onions and cook, stirring frequently, for 30 minutes, until deeply caramelized. Add the bay leaves and garlic, increase the heat to medium-high, and cook for another minute, until the bay leaves and garlic are fragrant. Add the water, bring to a boil over high heat, then reduce to a simmer. Cook for another 30 minutes. Strain liquid through a fine-mesh strainer set over a bowl. Discard the solids. Season the broth with salt to taste. (Broth can be made several days ahead and refrigerated, or frozen for several months.)

PICKLED SULTANAS Place all the ingredients in a small nonreactive saucepan. Simmer for 4 minutes, or until the raisins have plumped just above the level of the liquid. (Pickled sultanas will keep, refrigerated, for 1 week.)

CHARRED ONIONS Combine the onions, oil, and salt in a large mixing bowl and toss until evenly coated.

Heat a cast-iron pan over medium-high heat. Place the onions, cut side down, and cook for 5 minutes, or until the bottoms are charred. Add the sherry and water, stirring to scrape up any browned bits. Cover and simmer over low heat for 15 to 20 minutes, until the onions are tender. Remove the onions to a plate and allow to cool. Cut out the root ends and quarter the cipollinis.

ASSEMBLY Bring a large pot of water to a simmer and salt generously.

Meanwhile, in a large sauté pan set over medium-low heat, gently heat the laurel broth. Strain the sultanas and add to the broth along with the quartered cippolinis.

Working in batches, cook the frozen ravioli in the simmering water for 10 minutes, until they begin to float and the filling is warm. Remove with a slotted spoon and place in the sauté pan with the laurel broth.

Warm four serving bowls. Using a slotted spoon, place five ravioli in each. Top with sultanas and cippolinis from the broth. Ladle the laurel broth evenly among the bowls. Using a truffle shaver or coarse Micro-plane, shave toasted walnuts on the top and drizzle over the peppery olive oil. Serve.

DIJON VINAIGRETTE

¼ cup white wine vinegar

2 Tbsp Dijon mustard

¾ cup canola oil

Salt

ALLIUM CREAM

2 Tbsp unsalted butter

2 onions, chopped (3 cups)

1 ½ tsp salt

1 cup whole milk

½ cup heavy cream

1 bay leaf

2 to 3 tsp squid ink (see Note)

Smoked Black Cod with Charred Leeks and Blackened Radishes *Serves 4*

You don't need a special outdoor smoker to prepare this elegant entrée. A piece of foil, a few wood chips, and an oven will do the trick. Make sure you have adequate ventilation in your kitchen, either with a hood vent or a fan and an open window. Oven smoking, when done properly, produces a good deal of smoke when the oven door gets opened.

Note: Squid ink can be found in some gourmet markets and through online retailers. It is often either sealed in small, shelf-stable packets or refrigerated or frozen in small jars.

DIJON VINAIGRETTE In a small bowl, whisk together the vinegar and mustard. While whisking continuously, gradually add the oil in a thin, steady stream until emulsified. Taste and season with salt if necessary. (The vinaigrette can be made several days ahead.)

ALLIUM CREAM Melt the butter in a large saucepan over medium heat. Add the onions and salt, cover, and cook for 5 minutes, or until the onions have softened. Add the milk, cream, and bay leaf and simmer, uncovered, for 20 minutes, or until the onions are

completely tender and the mixture has reduced slightly.

Allow the mixture to cool slightly, remove the bay leaf, and strain the liquid into a bowl through a fine-mesh strainer.

Combine the onions and 2 teaspoons of the squid ink in a blender, add some of the strained cooking liquid, and purée until velvety in texture. Add more squid ink if necessary to achieve a dark color. Taste and adjust seasoning with additional salt if needed. Set aside. (The cream can be made several days ahead and refrigerated. Gently warm in a pot set over medium heat before use.)

CHARRED LEEKS AND BLACKENED RADISHES Preheat oven to 350°F. Heat oil and butter in a large cast-iron skillet or carbon steel pan over medium heat. Place leek rings and halved radishes cut side down in one even layer. Increase the heat to high and allow leeks and radishes to caramelize deeply on the bottom side, about 7 minutes.

Turn off the heat, carefully pour in the wine, and season with salt. Place the pan in the oven and cook for 10 to 20 minutes, until the

CHARRED LEEKS AND
BLACKENED RADISHES

2 Tbsp canola oil

2 Tbsp unsalted butter

2 large leeks, white and light green
  parts, cut into 1-inch-thick rings

10 small white or black radishes,
  trimmed and cut in half
  (or in quarters if large)

1 cup white wine

1 tsp salt

SMOKED BLACK COD

4 (4 oz) black cod fillets, gently scored
  on the skin

2 tsp salt

2 Tbsp wood chips (preferably alder)

4 Tbsp (½ stick) unsalted butter

ASSEMBLY

12 Belgian endive leaves,
  leaves separated

leeks and radishes are tender and the liquid has reduced to a glaze. Set aside. (This can be made several days ahead and refrigerated. Gently warm in a pot set over medium heat before use.)

SMOKED BLACK COD Preheat oven to 350°F. Season each fillet on all sides with salt and set aside for 5 minutes while the salt penetrates the flesh.

Meanwhile, make a small cup using a double layer of heavy-duty foil and fill with the wood chips.

Arrange the fish and cup of wood chips in the center of a 9- × 13-inch baking dish. Top each fillet with 1 tablespoon of butter. Using a lighter or kitchen torch, ignite the wood chips, blow out the flames, and allow them to smolder.

Immediately wrap the entire pan with foil and place in the oven for 7 minutes. Carefully remove the pan from the oven, uncover, and baste each fillet with pan juices. Bring the chips back to a smolder, cover the dish, and bake for another 5 minutes. Remove from the oven, baste the fish once more, and check the

cod for doneness by gently squeezing the fish. It should start to flake apart at the natural separations of the fish. If not, return to the oven until done.

ASSEMBLY Warm four plates (and the vegetables and cream if necessary). In a medium bowl, lightly dress the endive leaves in a few tablespoons of the Dijon vinaigrette.

Place one large spoonful of the warm allium cream on one side of each warmed plate. Using the back of the spoon, smear the cream diagonally in a straight line across the plate. Place a cod fillet at the tail end of the swipe of cream. Arrange the warm leeks and radishes around the cod portions. Place three dressed endive leaves on each plate among the radishes and leeks. Drizzle a small amount of vinaigrette around each cod portion and serve.

CARRIE ELLEN
PLAZA DEL TORO

WHEN YOU'RE THE lead pastry chef for seven restaurants that span a world of cuisines, it helps to have a globe-trotting history. Chef Carrie Ellen was born in Lisbon, Portugal, was raised in the small town of Monteagle, Tennessee, grew up to bake cakes in rural Suffolk, England, and eventually settled back in the States, where she honed her baking chops at Wolfgang Puck's CUT and Postrio restaurants in Las Vegas before settling in Portland for the long haul.

With Ellen's combination of talent and experience, it's no surprise chef-restaurateur John Gorham tapped her to run the pastry program for his growing restaurant empire. Tasked with developing desserts for all seven of his restaurants, her repertoire has to go the distance, dishing up classic Americana at Tasty n Sons, Middle Eastern delights at

Mediterranean Exploration Company, and Spanish sweets at Toro Bravo.

But it's at Gorham's "gastronomic society," the swanky PLAZA DEL TORO event space, where the pastry team can pull out all the stops for its ever-changing lineup of events. Gorham envisioned the Plaza as a culinary playground and never-ending dinner party, which is why every week brings something new. Sherry and tapas one night might be followed by a cooking competition between local chefs the next. But one thing stays the same— you can always count on a sweet finish.

Pictured: Chocolate Caramel Tart

Chocolate Caramel Tart *Serves 8*
(makes one 9-inch tart)

Buttery pastry filled with salted caramel and rich chocolate custard? Yes, please. This decadent beauty is a longtime menu favorite at Tasty n Sons, where it's served in adorable individual-size portions. Here it's presented in a dramatic full-size tart, perfect for special occasions.

PASTRY Using a stand mixer or hand mixer, combine the flour and sugar on low speed. Add the butter and continue mixing on low until the butter is broken into barely visible pieces. In a small bowl, whisk together the yolk and cream. With the mixer on low, drizzle the liquid ingredients into the dry and mix until the dough comes together. Turn the dough out onto a clean, dry work surface. Press together to make a ball, shape into a disk, wrap in plastic, and refrigerate overnight.

Sprinkle a clean, dry work surface with flour. Roll the dough into a circle about ¼-inch thick, continuously turning the dough a quarter turn and flouring as necessary whenever it starts to stick to the surface or the rolling pin. Transfer to a 9-inch tart pan with a removable bottom and press into the bottom and up the sides. Run a rolling pin across the top to trim the excess dough evenly with the rim. Freeze for 30 minutes. (Tart shell can be made a day ahead and refrigerated, or frozen for longer storage.)

Preheat oven to 325°F. Line the chilled tart shell with parchment paper and fill with rice, dried beans, or pie weights. Bake for 15 minutes, or until the crust is set and no longer raw. Remove the pie weights and paper and bake for another 10 to 15 minutes, until lightly golden. (The shell can be baked up to 2 days ahead and kept, wrapped, at room temperature.)

PASTRY

1 ¾ cups all-purpose flour

¼ cup granulated sugar

½ cup (1 stick) plus 3 Tbsp
   cold unsalted butter, diced

1 egg yolk

1 Tbsp heavy cream

CARAMEL FILLING

⅓ cup light corn syrup

2 cups granulated sugar

½ cup (1 stick) cold unsalted
   butter, diced

¾ cup heavy cream

2 Tbsp sour cream

¼ tsp salt

CHOCOLATE FILLING

7 ½ oz dark chocolate, 60% or higher,
   chopped

3 Tbsp plus 1 tsp granulated sugar

2 egg yolks

½ cup whole milk

½ cup heavy cream

Flaky sea salt, for garnish

CARAMEL FILLING Heat the corn syrup in a large saucepan set over medium-high heat, stirring occasionally, until warm and fluid. Add the sugar in batches, stirring each batch until dissolved before adding more. Increase heat to high and bring to a boil. Cook, swirling the pan occasionally to promote even cooking, until the mixture is caramel in color and reaches 245°F on a candy thermometer (do not stir during this time or the sugar might crystallize). Remove from heat and whisk in the butter, cream, and sour cream until smooth (be careful, the mixture will bubble furiously). Stir in the salt. Pour the caramel into the tart shell, filling it about halfway. Set aside to cool.

CHOCOLATE FILLING Place the chocolate in a heatproof bowl and set over a saucepan of water. Bring the water to a simmer, turn off the heat, and let the chocolate sit until it is melted, stirring occasionally until smooth. Set aside.

In a separate bowl, mix together the sugar and egg yolks. In a medium saucepan, combine the milk and cream. Bring just to a boil over medium-high heat. Remove from the heat and gradually pour about a third of the hot milk mixture into the yolk mixture, whisking vigorously (this tempers the eggs and keeps them from curdling). Pour the yolk mixture back into the pot and set over medium-low heat. Whisking gently and continuously, cook until the custard thickens and reaches a temperature of 170°F.

Gently fold the custard into the melted chocolate, trying not to incorporate too much air. Pour the chocolate filling over the cooled caramel filling in the tart and refrigerate for 30 minutes, or until set. Sprinkle with flaky sea salt and bring back to room temperature before serving.

INGREDIENTS

6 egg yolks

⅓ cup plus 1 Tbsp malted milk powder

2 ½ cups whole milk

1 cup heavy cream

¾ cup granulated sugar

⅛ tsp salt

4 oz milk chocolate, chopped

Malted Milk Chocolate Ice Cream *Serves 4 to 6*

Chocolate malt lovers, you've just met the ice cream of your dreams. It's like a scoop-able version of your favorite milkshake and phenomenal topped with hot fudge and crushed malt balls.

METHOD Mix the yolks and malt powder together in a large bowl and set aside. In a medium saucepan, whisk together the milk, cream, sugar, and salt. Bring just to a boil over medium-high heat, stirring frequently. Remove from the heat and gradually whisk about a third of the hot cream mixture into the bowl of yolks (this tempers the eggs and keeps them from curdling). Pour the yolk mixture back into the pot and set over low heat. Whisking gently and continuously, cook until it reaches 175°F.

Set the chocolate in a large bowl. Pour the hot custard mixture through a fine-mesh strainer set over the bowl of chocolate. Allow it to melt the chocolate, then mix thoroughly. Cool until room temperature, then cover with plastic wrap and refrigerate overnight. (Do not refrigerate the custard while hot. If you need to chill the mixture in a hurry, set the bowl into a larger bowl filled with ice.)

Churn the ice cream in an ice cream maker according to the manufacturer's instructions until it's the texture of soft-serve. Transfer the ice cream to an airtight container and freeze for at least 12 hours to harden before serving.

Kachka

ANNIE CUGGINO

Q Restaurant and Bar

IN 1994, long before Portland was even a blip on the culinary radar, chef Annie Cuggino arrived fresh from stints at Union Square Cafe in New York and Emeril's in New Orleans and turned a quaint pub called Veritable Quandary into a bona fide dining destination. With Cuggino at the helm, it held a top spot in local restaurant guides for years and gained a large and loyal following of regulars in the process. But she has since started a new chapter, stepping out from behind the scenes to take center stage in the open kitchen at Q Restaurant and Bar.

At the buzzy new space, Cuggino continues to cook some of the most beloved dishes in town, including refined classics like osso buco and addictively glazed bacon-wrapped dates — a longtime must-order that's just the thing with a predinner martini. Although she's stocked the new menu with many of her greatest hits — dishes so adored she couldn't take them off even if she tried — she's introduced a new category of favorites thanks to the addition of an in-house smoker. As she masterfully weaves smoke-kissed ingredients like duck breast, cheese, and vegetables into her dishes, Cuggino is expanding her repertoire of inventive Northwest cuisine and earning a whole new cadre of fans in the process.

INGREDIENTS

12 Deglet Noor dates, pitted

¼ cup chèvre (preferably Cypress Grove)

12 Marcona almonds, toasted

2 tsp freshly ground black pepper

6 slices high-quality meaty bacon,
 cut in half

1 ½ cups sweet Marsala wine

4 (6-inch) bamboo skewers

Bacon-Wrapped Dates *Serves 4*

Chef Annie Cuggino's bacon-wrapped dates drizzled in a luscious Marsala reduction are an easy and elegant appetizer. Look for bacon with a lot of meat, but be sure it's not thick-cut. Although Cuggino crisps her dates on the grill, most of us will opt for the ease of the broiler.

METHOD Preheat broiler or outdoor grill to medium-high heat. Set a large sauté pan over medium heat and cook the bacon until cooked through but not crispy.

Stuff each date with 1 teaspoon chèvre and 1 almond. Sprinkle liberally with pepper. Wrap each date with a piece of bacon, then thread onto a skewer, placing three stuffed dates on each skewer. (They can be made a day ahead and refrigerated.) Arrange the skewered dates on a baking sheet and broil or grill for 5 minutes, turning over once during cooking, until crisp.

Meanwhile, pour the Marsala into a medium saucepan and bring to a boil over high heat. Boil for about 12 minutes, or until reduced to ¼ cup and thick enough to coat a spoon (it will thicken a bit more as it cools).

Arrange the broiled dates on plates or a serving platter. Drizzle with the reduced Marsala and serve.

GREMOLATA

Zest of 1 lemon

4 cloves garlic, finely chopped

¼ cup finely chopped fresh
   Italian parsley

OSSO BUCO

4 (14 oz) cross-cut veal shanks

Salt and freshly ground black
   pepper

1 cup all-purpose flour

2 Tbsp extra-virgin olive oil

2 onions, diced

2 carrots, diced

3 stalks celery, diced

6 cloves garlic, finely chopped

750 ml bottle red wine, such as Merlot

3 to 4 sprigs fresh rosemary, leaves
   removed and chopped

2 to 3 cups homemade beef stock

28 oz can whole Italian tomatoes,
   such as Rega or Cento brands

Cooked risotto, to serve

Grated Pecorino Romano, for serving

Osso Buco

Serves 4

Although it's tradition to serve these rich veal shanks alongside saffron risotto, chef Annie Cuggino goes a more decadent route, enriching her risotto with copious amounts of Parmesan. You'd be wise to follow suit.

GREMOLATA Combine all the ingredients in a small bowl and stir.

OSSO BUCO Generously season the veal shanks with salt and pepper. Allow to sit for 1 to 2 hours, or refrigerate overnight.

Place the flour in a shallow bowl and add the shanks, one at a time, turning to coat. Shake off the excess.

Heat the oil in a 6-quart oven-safe Dutch oven set over medium-high heat. Sear the shanks for 10 minutes, or until browned on all sides. Transfer to a plate. Add the onions, carrots, and celery and sauté for 5 minutes, until softened. Add the garlic and sauté for another minute. Pour in the wine, stirring to scrape the browned bits. Place the shanks back in the pot along with the rosemary. Pour in just enough beef stock to cover. Lightly crush the tomatoes, then pour them over the shanks along with their juices.

(Putting the tomatoes on top will keep the shanks moist and they'll deepen in flavor from being exposed to the heat of the oven.)

Preheat oven to 250°F. Bring the osso buco to a simmer over medium-high heat, then transfer to the oven. Cook, uncovered, for 3 hours, until shanks are tender but not completely falling apart. (Periodically check to make sure that the top is not too brown and that the sauce is slightly simmering.) You may have to give it a few stirs, but some browning is good.

Remove the meat from the sauce and set aside. Allow sauce to settle until the fat rises to the top, then skim it off. Set the pot over medium-high heat and bring the sauce to a simmer. Cook for 15 minutes, until slightly thickened. Return the shanks to the sauce and simmer until heated through.

Divide the shanks among four plates, ladle some of the sauce over the meat, sprinkle with gremolata and Pecorino Romano, and serve with risotto.

DANIEL MONDOK & LISA MYGRANT

Raven & Rose

WHEN LISA MYGRANT decides to do something, she doesn't just dip a toe, she goes all in. Case in point: Raven & Rose. She didn't just open her first restaurant in a charming old building; she opened it in a 7,000-square-foot, 130-year-old historic landmark. And she didn't just renovate it first; she completely restored it, to LEED Gold–certified standards. And when she launched Raven & Rose in the Ladd Carriage House in early 2013, she didn't go with the prevailing trends and open, say, a Neapolitan-style pizza joint; she chose a cuisine befitting the age and tenor of the place: the rustic-elegant dishes of the British Isles.

And though she has prestigious restaurant experience of her own (Ballymaloe Cookery School in Ireland and Berkeley's famed Chez Panisse), she's wisely hired some of the heaviest hitters in town to guide the food

and drinks. Chef Daniel Mondok earned his stripes at places like The French Laundry and Elisabeth Daniel in San Francisco and has led the kitchens in some of Portland's top restaurants. At Raven & Rose, he uses his deep connections with Willamette Valley farmers to create a locally sourced, seasonal menu that's grounded in tradition and works in tandem with bar manager David Shenaut's award-winning wine list. Think double-cut pork chops from family-owned Worden Hill Farm served alongside housemade "HP" sauce, or shepherd's pie with tender chunks of braised lamb from Reister Farms. It's a menu that offers food with a sense of place, and time, thanks to Mondok's skill and Mygrant's vision.

Pictured: Shepherd's Pie

2 ½ lb grass-fed beef chuck or lamb
  shoulder, trimmed and cut into
  ¾-inch cubes
Salt and freshly ground black
  pepper
3 Tbsp vegetable oil
¼ cup all-purpose flour

2 cups dark beer, such as stout
  or porter
3 cups rich beef, chicken, or lamb stock
1 large carrot, cut into chunks
1 stalk celery, cut into chunks
½ large onion, cut into chunks
2 cloves garlic
1 sprig fresh thyme

Shepherd's Pie

Serves 8

At Raven & Rose, shepherd's pie is sometimes made with lamb, other times with beef (which means it's technically cottage pie). No matter the variation, it's always made with meltingly tender, long-braised cuts instead of ground meats. Don't be afraid to go off course and try other vegetables, and you can mix up the mash with sliced scallions, herbs, buttermilk, or cheddar.

STEW Season meat generously with salt and pepper. Set aside at room temperature for up to 1 hour or refrigerate for up to 2 days.

Preheat oven to 325°F. Heat the oil in a 6-quart oven-safe Dutch oven set over medium-high heat. Working in batches to avoid crowding, sear the meat in an even layer until browned on all sides, about 3 minutes per side.

Sprinkle the flour over the browned meat and cook, stirring, for about 5 minutes. Reduce heat to low and add the beer, stirring to scrape up the browned bits. Add the stock, vegetables, garlic cloves, and thyme sprig.

Cover, place in the oven, and cook for about 3 hours, stirring occasionally to make sure the mixture isn't sticking to the bottom of the pot or drying out. (Add a splash of water or stock, as needed, if liquid is too thick.) The meat is done when it is falling-apart tender. Discard the vegetable chunks and thyme sprig.

CARAMELIZED VEGETABLES

¼ cup (½ stick) unsalted butter

1 ½ large onions, diced

Salt and freshly ground black pepper

3 large carrots, diced

3 stalks celery, diced

4 cloves garlic, finely chopped

2 Tbsp chopped fresh thyme

1 Tbsp Worcestershire sauce

2 Tbsp tomato paste

2 tsp dry mustard

MASHED POTATOES

4 large russet potatoes, peeled and cut into quarters

¼ cup (½ stick) unsalted butter, melted

½ cup half-and-half, warmed, plus more if needed

Salt and freshly ground black pepper

ASSEMBLY

2 Tbsp finely chopped fresh Italian parsley or chives, for garnish

Green salad and warm bread, to serve

CARAMELIZED VEGETABLES Melt the butter in a large sauté pan over medium heat. Add the diced onions, season with salt and pepper, and sauté for 10 minutes, until soft and just starting to brown. Add the diced carrots and celery, season again, and sauté for another 10 to 12 minutes, until the vegetables are just cooked through and are starting to brown. Adjust heat as necessary to avoid burning. Add the chopped garlic and cook for another minute.

Transfer vegetables to the pot with the braised meat. Add the chopped thyme, Worcestershire sauce, tomato paste, and dry mustard. Bring to a simmer over medium-low heat and cook for 10 minutes. Taste and adjust seasonings if desired.

MASHED POTATOES Place the potatoes in a large pot and cover with water by 1 inch. Salt generously. Bring to a boil over medium-high heat, reduce to a simmer, and cook for 10 minutes, until easily pierced with a fork.

Drain and return to the pot. Mash with a potato masher or pass through a food mill or potato ricer. Add the melted butter and stir until incorporated. Gradually add the half-and-half, beating with a wooden spoon as you go, until fully incorporated. Add a little more cream if desired. Season with salt and pepper to taste.

ASSEMBLY Preheat broiler. Divide the stew among several individual baking dishes or large ramekins, or transfer to a large baking dish (or just leave it in the Dutch oven). Pipe or scoop the mashed potatoes over the top of the stew, covering it completely. Place briefly in the oven under the broiler just to brown the tops of the potatoes. (Watch carefully to avoid burning.)

To serve, sprinkle freshly chopped herbs over the top. Serve with a fresh green salad and warm bread with Irish butter.

Butterscotch Pudding *Serves 6*

From the day Raven & Rose opened, this decadent pudding was an instant hit, and it has remained on the menu since. It's totally delicious on its own, but the restaurant takes it over the top with butterscotch sauce, softly whipped cream, and a sprinkle of crispy streusel.

PUDDING In a medium saucepan over medium-high heat, combine the dark brown sugar, salt, and water. Cook for 6 to 8 minutes, to firm-ball stage (248°F on a candy thermometer). Remove from heat and slowly but steadily whisk in the milk and cream. Return to medium heat and bring to a gentle simmer. Watch carefully, as it can boil over quickly.

Meanwhile, in a large mixing bowl, whisk together the egg, yolks, granulated sugar, and cornstarch until smooth. As soon as the first small bubbles appear in the milk mixture, remove from heat and slowly whisk the hot milk into the egg mixture. (This will temper the eggs, preventing them from scrambling.) Return the mixture to the saucepan and cook over low heat, whisking continuously, just until mixture thickens and barely bubbles. (Avoid a full rolling boil, as it will scorch and/or curdle.) Remove from heat and whisk in the butter and vanilla. Cool to room temperature. (Optional: To avoid a skin forming on top of the pudding during cooling, pour into a stand mixer with a paddle attachment and mix on low until it has cooled to room temperature.)

Strain the pudding through a fine-mesh strainer into ramekins or jelly jars. Cover with plastic wrap or lids and chill until set, several hours or overnight.

PUDDING

⅔ cup packed dark brown sugar

1 tsp salt

¼ cup water

1 cup plus 1 Tbsp whole milk

2 cups plus 2 Tbsp heavy cream

1 egg

2 egg yolks

2 Tbsp plus 1 ½ tsp granulated sugar

3 Tbsp cornstarch

¼ cup (½ stick) unsalted butter,
  cut into cubes

1 tsp pure vanilla extract

Softly whipped cream, to serve

BUTTERSCOTCH SAUCE

¼ cup (½ stick) unsalted butter

¼ cup packed dark brown sugar

¼ cup granulated sugar

¼ cup corn syrup

1 Tbsp water

3 Tbsp heavy cream

¼ tsp pure vanilla extract

Pinch of salt

STREUSEL

1 cup all-purpose flour

½ cup (1 stick) cold unsalted butter,
  cut into cubes

¼ cup granulated sugar

¼ cup packed brown sugar

½ tsp salt

¼ tsp ground cinnamon

BUTTERSCOTCH SAUCE In a small saucepan, combine all the ingredients, bring to a simmer over medium heat, and cook for 4 to 5 minutes, or until emulsified. Strain through a fine-mesh strainer and refrigerate until ready to use.

STREUSEL Preheat oven to 375°F. Place all the ingredients into a food processor and pulse until the mixture resembles fine crumbs. Sprinkle on a parchment-lined baking sheet and bake until golden and crisp, about 10 minutes. Cool completely, then store in an airtight container until ready to use.

TO SERVE Top each pudding with whipped cream and butterscotch sauce, and sprinkle with crispy streusel.

DAVID SHENAUT & LISA MYGRANT

The Rookery Bar

JUDGING BY THE gingerbread details of the 130-year-old Ladd Carriage House, you'd probably expect it to be home to a high-end antique store, not one of the most ambitious bars in Portland. It turns out, though, that The Rookery Bar, tucked upstairs above its sister restaurant, Raven & Rose, is guided by some of the city's most talented bartenders. Beverage director David Shenaut made his name at several of Portland's most cutting-edge bars — Teardrop, Beaker & Flask, Kask — and he brought that same level of detail, experimentation, collaboration, and expertise when he launched the beverage program at The Rookery Bar. Using the building itself as inspiration, he designed a thoroughly modern cocktail list that still somehow fits in seamlessly with the vintage of the place.

Everything is housemade, from the bitters to the brandied cherries, just as it would be in the 1880s, and there's an emphasis on American-made spirits like bourbon, bought by the barrel just like in the old days.

But even with its serious dedication to historical details — both on the menu and in the leather-clad, billiards-club décor — The Rookery Bar is downright fun. With live music, playful drinks, collaborative events, and holiday parties, it's clear Shenaut and owner Lisa Mygrant are dedicated to building a community on both sides of the bar.

INGREDIENTS

¾ oz rye whiskey

¾ oz Campari

¾ oz Cocchi Vermouth di Torino

¾ oz freshly squeezed lime juice

Ice

1 oz spicy ginger beer

1 lime wheel

Souracher

Serves 1

David Shenaut has been perfecting this original recipe while working behind several different bars over the years. His most recent version is the best yet — a light, refreshing cocktail that can be served all year as an aperitif or in hot weather as a porch sipper.

METHOD Combine the rye, Campari, vermouth, and lime juice in a cocktail shaker filled with ice. Shake vigorously until condensation forms on the outside. Strain into a Collins glass filled with fresh ice and top with ginger beer. Garnish with a lime wheel and serve with a straw.

Ice

2 ¼ oz single-barrel bourbon

4 dashes of Angostura bitters

1 dash of Regans' orange bitters

1 dash of Fee Brothers' orange bitters

¼ oz muscovado syrup (see Note)

Large ice cube, for serving

1 wide strip fresh orange peel,
   2 to 3 inches long

Sim's Old Fashioned

Serves 1

The Rookery Bar's Sim's Old Fashioned is its most popular item of any sort — food or drink. The muscovado syrup is the secret, so don't be tempted to substitute a different sugar. However, you can experiment with any number of bourbon whiskeys. The fresh orange oil makes a huge difference to the experience and shouldn't be skipped.

Note: To make the muscovado syrup, combine 1 cup packed dark brown muscovado sugar (preferably India Tree brand) with ½ cup water in a small saucepan set over medium-low heat. Gently warm until the sugar dissolves and is no longer granular. (Do not boil.) Allow to cool completely before using. Syrup will keep refrigerated for several weeks.

METHOD In a mixing glass filled with ice, combine the bourbon, both bitters, and the muscovado syrup. Stir until cold. Strain into a short tumbler filled with a very large ice cube (to minimize dilution). Hold the orange peel over the cocktail and lightly squeeze it along its midline to express the aromatic oils into the glass. Rub it over the glass rim, then drop it into the drink.

TYLER MALEK

Salt & Straw | Wiz Bang Bar

IT WASN'T ENOUGH to be Portland's first farm-to-cone ice cream shop. Cousins and business partners Tyler and Kim Malek just had to take their local-first agenda to the absolute limit. They not only source locally grown ingredients, they also pair them with locally made products, from olive oil to cocktail bitters. And they don't stop there; they also tap into the local talent pool, collaborating with chefs to produce ice cream flavors that boggle the mind. Foie Gras S'mores, and Fish Sauce Caramel with Kaffir Lime and Lemongrass are just a couple of drops in Salt & Straw's ever-changing sea of flavors, which is powered by Tyler's seemingly boundless curiosity, energy, and madcap ingenuity.

But no matter how out-there the flavors get, local is still key, which is why Salt & Straw's expansion into California came complete with its own lineup of Golden State–inspired flavors. And Wiz Bang Bar, Salt & Straw's year-old sundae emporium in Pine Street Market, serves up things like soft-serve steeped in Portland's Steven Smith tea and housemade magic shell blended with Oregon berries.

For Tyler, ice cream truly is a canvas. A blank slate. Not an end product, but a vehicle for creativity. The volume of boundary-pushing flavors that rotates monthly through Salt & Straw's charming Portland shops is staggering—as are the ever-present long lines of people waiting to try them. But your wait is rewarded with patient staff who will happily offer samples of every single flavor and, ultimately, hand you a rich and creamy scoop that you just can't get anywhere else.

Goat Cheese Ice Cream with
Marionberry-Habanero Ribbons

Goat Cheese Ice Cream with Marionberry-Habanero Ribbons *Serves 4 to 6*

Tyler says that of the hundreds of ice cream flavors he's made, this is one of his absolute favorites. He stirs tangy, creamy, ultrafresh Portland Creamery goat cheese into the base and ribbons the ice cream with a sweet, yet fiery, marionberry jam. The more seeds you leave in the habaneros, the hotter the jam will be, though it mellows quite a bit when frozen.

Note: Xanthan gum helps keep ice cream from forming ice crystals, which would ruin its smooth and creamy texture. It's often used in gluten-free baking, so look for it in the baking aisle or near gluten-free products. Bob's Red Mill is a common brand.

ICE CREAM BASE Combine the sugar and xanthan gum in a small bowl. Combine the milk, evaporated milk, and corn syrup in a medium pot (off the heat). Whisking vigorously, slowly mix the sugar mixture into the milk. Don't worry if the xanthan gum causes a few lumps, but try to whisk hard enough to get the sugar and xanthan gum mixed evenly.

Set the pot over medium heat and cook, stirring constantly, just until the mixture is hot and the sugar is completely dissolved. (Try to avoid simmering—you're just trying to melt the sugar and give the xanthan gum a head start in activating.) Allow the milk mixture to cool to room temperature.

Stir in the cream and refrigerate until well chilled, at least overnight but preferably 24 to 48 hours for a better texture and milkier flavor.

¾ cup granulated sugar

¼ tsp xanthan gum (see Note)

1 ¼ cups whole milk

¾ cup canned evaporated milk

2 Tbsp light corn syrup

1 ¾ cups heavy cream

MARIONBERRY-HABANERO JAM

1 cup marionberries

½ habanero pepper, ribs and seeds removed if desired, chopped

2 tsp freshly squeezed lemon juice

1 Tbsp plus 1 ½ tsp powdered pectin

½ cup granulated sugar

ASSEMBLY

1 cup (8 oz) goat cheese, softened

1 tsp kosher salt

1 Tbsp freshly squeezed lemon juice

⅔ cup marionberry-habanero jam (see here)

MARIONBERRY-HABANERO JAM

Combine the berries, habanero, lemon juice, and pectin in a pot, smashing the berries to release some juices. Cook over medium-high heat, stirring occasionally, until the mixture begins to simmer. Stir in the sugar, bring the berries back to a simmer, and cook for another minute.

Remove from heat and purée with a hand blender, food processor, or regular blender with the lid ajar, or just mash thoroughly with a whisk. While still hot, strain through a fine-mesh strainer to remove the seeds. Refrigerate overnight.

ASSEMBLY Mix the ice cream base with goat cheese and salt, mashing as needed to break the cheese up into the cream. Add lemon juice to the ice cream base and immediately transfer to the ice cream maker. Churn the ice cream base according to the manufacturer's instructions until it's the texture of soft-serve.

Using a spoon or ice cream spade, transfer the ice cream to an airtight container, half a scoop at a time, layering it with a generous spoonful of cold marionberry-habanero jam as you go (work quickly so the ice cream doesn't melt). This is where a lot of the artistry of ice cream making comes into play, as you try to achieve the perfect ratio of ice cream to jam for each scoop. (You might not use all the jam. You can refrigerate the remainder for several weeks.)

Flip the container upside down and store in the coldest part of your freezer for at least 12 hours to harden before serving. (We flip the container so that it'll create an airtight seal on the top, keeping the ice cream super-fresh.) When ready to serve, allow the ice cream to sit out at room temperature for about 5 minutes until scoopable.

Mock Apple Pie with Candied Apples *Serves 8*

When Salt & Straw opened Wiz Bang Bar—
its sundae and soft-serve extravaganza in the
Pine Street Market food hall—Tyler Malek's
version of a mock apple pie made with Ritz
crackers blew everyone's mind. He gives the
age-old recipe a decadent overhaul with a
custardy filling that echoes the scoop of ice
cream he serves on top.

CANDIED APPLES Heat the sugar and
water in a small saucepan over medium-
high heat until sugar dissolves. Allow to
cool. Add the apple juice and lemon juice.
Peel and core the apples, then slice them
into ⅛-inch-thick slices, preferably on a
mandoline. Add the apples to the syrup
and refrigerate for at least 4 hours and
up to 1 week.

PIE SHELL Combine the flour, salt, and sugar
in a food processor and pulse to combine.
Add the butter and pulse until the mixture
looks like coarse cornmeal with a few larger
pieces. While pulsing, drizzle in the ice-cold
water and vodka (which helps make the
dough tender), until the mixture starts to
come together. Stop and squeeze the mixture.
It should hold together without crumbling
apart, but not feel wet or sticky. Add more
water if necessary. Turn the dough out onto a
clean, dry surface and gather it together into
a ball. Form into a disk, wrap in plastic, and
refrigerate for at least 2 hours or overnight.

Sprinkle a clean, dry work surface with
flour. Roll the dough into a circle about
12 inches in diameter and ⅛ inch thick,
continuously turning the dough a quarter
turn and flouring as necessary whenever
it starts to stick to the surface or the rolling
pin. Transfer to a 9-inch pie dish. Trim the
dough to ½ inch over the rim, fold the edges
under, and crimp. Refrigerate or freeze for
30 minutes. (The shell can be made a day
ahead and refrigerated, or frozen for longer
storage.)

CANDIED APPLES

1 cup granulated sugar

1 cup water

1 Tbsp apple juice

1 Tbsp freshly squeezed
  lemon juice

2 tart apples

PIE SHELL

1 ¼ cups all-purpose flour, plus
  more for rolling

½ tsp kosher salt

1 Tbsp granulated sugar

½ cup (1 stick) cold unsalted
  butter, cut into ½-inch cubes

2 Tbsp cup ice-cold water

2 Tbsp vodka

MOCK APPLE PIE FILLING

½ cup (1 stick) unsalted butter

⅓ cup honey

⅓ cup light corn syrup

½ cup granulated sugar

3 eggs

½ cup heavy cream

2 tsp white vinegar

1 tsp pure vanilla extract

1 ¼ rolls Ritz crackers (about 43 crackers)

ASSEMBLY

Salted caramel or vanilla ice cream

Preheat oven to 425°F. Line the chilled pie shell with parchment paper and fill with pie weights, rice, or dried beans. Bake for 15 minutes, or until the crust is set and no longer raw. Remove the pie weights and paper and bake for another 10 to 15 minutes, until lightly golden. (The shell can be baked up to 2 days ahead and kept, wrapped, at room temperature.)

MOCK APPLE PIE FILLING Preheat oven to 350°F. Melt the butter in a small saucepan over medium-low heat. Remove from heat and stir in the honey, corn syrup, and sugar until combined. Whisk in the eggs, cream, vinegar, and vanilla until smooth. (It can be made up to 3 days ahead and refrigerated.)

In a bowl, lightly crush the crackers or break in half. Try not to crush them too much — the goal is to leave them large enough so they look like apple slices after they're baked. Pour the egg mixture over the crackers and soak for 15 minutes, or until sufficiently soggy.

Use a slotted spoon to fill the pie shell with the soaked crackers. Pour the soaking liquid over the crackers until the pie shell is full.

Set on a rimmed baking sheet and bake for 40 to 50 minutes, until the top is golden brown and a knife inserted in the center comes out clean. Allow the pie to cool until warm, or chill overnight.

ASSEMBLY Cut the pie into eight slices and serve with a scoop of salted caramel or vanilla ice cream and a few slices of candied apples.

ALISE MOFFATT & ANNE GARCIA

Shift Drinks

YOU KNOW YOU'VE walked into an industry bar when it's named after the long-awaited drink that chefs and servers sit down to at the end of their shifts. But those are usually dive bars, where people get loud, blow off steam, and stretch their tips with cheap well drinks.

Shift Drinks is anything but. Sure, there's a long list of restaurant and bar friends the crew can count on as regulars. After all, owners Alise Moffatt and Anne and Anthony Garcia are industry kids themselves, having spent years working at many of Portland's best bars and restaurants. But this downtown hotspot isn't so much a watering hole for service professionals as a celebration of the industry itself. At the heart of this sleek cocktail den, with its grayscale modernity, is a genuine warmth and a core belief that there is beauty in hospitality and honor in providing it.

Though it's just two years old, Shift Drinks runs on the decades of experience and deep knowledge of fine wines, spirits, and food that each of the owners brings. Moffatt has helped open some of the city's best bars, including Multnomah Whiskey Library, and is known for crafting cocktails of elegance and distinction. Anthony Garcia is an advanced sommelier, who fills the bar's former bank vault with nerdy yet approachable bottles. And his wife, chef Anne Garcia, harnesses her knowledge of savory and sweet, creating a tight menu of seasonal, farm-fresh, and ingredient-focused small plates, generously served into the wee hours.

Pictured: Physically Forgotten

INGREDIENTS

2 large bulbs fennel

1 cup finely grated Grana Padano, plus extra for garnish

¼ cup oil-cured black olives (such as Beldi from Morocco), chopped

¼ cup dried Mission figs, cut into matchsticks

¼ cup chopped roasted hazelnuts (see Note)

1 Tbsp plus 1 ½ tsp freshly squeezed lemon juice

¼ cup extra-virgin olive oil

¼ tsp flaky sea salt (preferably Maldon or Jacobsen)

Freshly ground black pepper

Flavorful olive oil, for drizzling (optional)

Shaved Fennel Salad with Figs, Olives, and Hazelnuts *Serves 4*

Paper-thin slices of fresh fennel provide a subtly fragrant backdrop to bold, oil-cured olives, sweet dried figs, and earthy hazelnuts.

Note: You can often find roasted hazelnuts in the bulk bin at well-stocked supermarkets. To roast your own, spread raw hazelnuts in an even layer on a rimmed baking sheet and toast in a 350°F oven until beginning to darken and smell nutty, about 8 to 12 minutes. Transfer to a clean dish towel, gather the ends, and massage to remove most of the skins. Open carefully and separate the whole nuts from the dry skins.

METHOD Cut fennel crosswise into ⅛-inch-thick slices, preferably with a mandoline. You should have about 4 cups.

In a large mixing bowl, combine the fennel, cheese, olives, figs, and hazelnuts. Just before serving, add the lemon juice, olive oil, and salt and pepper to taste. Toss until thoroughly combined. Taste and add more lemon juice if desired.

Divide among four plates and garnish with more cheese and a drizzle of flavorful olive oil, if using.

1 ½ oz London dry gin

¾ oz Cynar

½ oz Luxardo maraschino liqueur

2 dashes of orange bitters

Ice

Lemon peel, for garnish

Physically Forgotten

Serves 1

Bartender Alise Moffatt is known for her exceptionally elegant drinks, and this beauty is no different. In it, she gives dry gin a bittersweet boost with Cynar and maraschino liqueur.

METHOD Combine the gin, Cynar, maraschino liqueur, and bitters in a mixing glass with ice and stir until chilled. Strain into a chilled coupe glass. Hold the lemon peel over the cocktail and lightly squeeze it along its midline to express the aromatic oils into the glass, then discard.

The Solo Club

The Solo Club

THERE'S A WHIFF OF the trade winds in almost everything about The Solo Club, from the Southeast Asian–inspired menu to the wicker-wrapped motorcycle hanging proudly above the stunning bar. But this ain't no Trader Vic's, not by a long shot. With its lofty ceiling and intricately patterned floor, the décor transports without ever feeling like a movie set. Instead of complicated tiki drinks, the cocktails veer toward simple three-ingredient sippers. And for the playful, there's a lineup of customizable "coolers," which pair a sparkler like cava, beer, or gin-spiked tonic with your choice of bitters or amari, from the vast selection curated by co-owner and local bitters aficionado Mark Bitterman.

That choose-your-own-adventure spirit is what The Solo Club is all about. The sister bar to Besaw's next door, it's flexible enough to be whatever you need it to be. It's your morning coffee stop, your casual lunch joint, your happy hour watering hole, your sexy date-night supperclub, or your post-concert dessert stop before heading home. The dinner menu is a complete departure from the farm-to-table fare chef/co-owner Dustin Clark created at Portland's iconic Wildwood, and certainly different from what he serves next door, but it's clearly driven by his own passion for the cuisine. Complementing his Burmese Chicken Salad and Goat Curry with Smoked Potatoes are expert desserts like Matcha Layer Cake by lauded pastry chef Michelle Vernier. You get a sense that the same adventurous spirit that makes The Solo Club so special is what drives the team behind it, too.

INGREDIENTS

1 oz Avèze gentian liqueur
1 oz Plantation Barbados 5-year rum
1 oz Yzaguirre Blanco Reserva vermouth
Ice

Dandelion Rum #2 *Serves 1*

The first thing you spot upon entering The Solo Club is its impressive bar decked out with intricate geometric carvings. Clearly cocktails are cause for celebration here, and this easy sipper is a prime example. Two liquors add the namesake's yellow color: the Spanish Yzaguirre Blanco Reserva vermouth, which is aged to velvety smoothness for a year in oak barrels, and Avèze gentian liqueur, with its bittersweet herbal flavor. The rum, aged in bourbon and cognac casks, adds notes of caramel. With its one-to-one-to-one ratio, it's easy to batch up a bunch of this cocktail to serve a crowd.

METHOD Combine the ingredients in a mixing glass with ice and stir with a bar spoon until chilled. Strain into a chilled Nick and Nora glass (similar to a long-stemmed coupe).

FRIED SHALLOTS AND SHALLOT OIL

½ cup canola oil
3 large shallots, thinly sliced
Salt

POACHING

1 lb boneless, skinless chicken breasts
1 clove garlic, smashed
1 carrot, cut into chunks
1 bay leaf
1 tsp whole black peppercorns
1 cup white wine

SALAD

1 large shallot, thinly sliced
Juice of 2 limes
1 Tbsp fish sauce (The Solo Club uses Red Boat brand)
½ tsp kosher salt
½ to 1 Thai red chile, seeded and finely chopped
½ cup coarsely chopped fresh mint leaves
½ cup coarsely chopped fresh cilantro
¼ cup coarsely chopped fresh Thai basil
⅓ cup finely chopped roasted peanuts

Burmese Chicken Salad *Serves 4*

Every bite of this vibrant salad bursts with bright, herbaceous flavors. In fact, you might never want to make the usual mayonnaise-based chicken salad ever again. The oil from the fried shallots is used in the dressing, but you'll have some left over. Do as the Burmese do and save the flavorful oil to use in other dishes, like stir-fries, or drizzle it as a finishing oil. Or you can cheat and buy a tub of fried shallots at the Asian market.

FRIED SHALLOTS AND SHALLOT OIL
Combine oil and shallots in a medium saucepan and set over medium heat. Cook, stirring frequently, until golden brown, about 10 minutes. Remove with a slotted spoon and transfer to paper towels to drain the excess oil. Season with salt.

Strain the oil through a fine-mesh strainer to remove any particles, and set both the fried shallots and the shallot oil aside.

POACHING Set chicken in an even layer in the bottom of a large saucepan. Add the garlic, carrot, bay leaf, peppercorns, and white wine. Add enough cold water to cover by 1 inch. Bring to a simmer over medium-high heat, reduce heat to medium-low, cover, and cook for 10 to 15 minutes, or until cooked through and temperature reads 160°F on a meat thermometer. Remove from heat and allow to cool in the liquid before cutting or tearing into bite-size chunks.

SALAD Place sliced shallots in a bowl and cover with cold water. Allow to soak for 10 minutes (this makes them fresh and crunchy with a less astringent flavor).

In a large bowl, whisk together lime juice, fish sauce, salt, 2 tablespoons of the reserved shallot oil, and chopped chile. Add cooked chicken and soaked shallots, tossing to coat. Allow to stand for 10 minutes. Taste and add more shallot oil or lime juice if desired. Add mint, cilantro, Thai basil, peanuts, and fried shallots. Toss to combine. Divide among plates and serve.

AARON BARNETT

St. Jack | La Moule

TO UNDERSTAND seven-year-old St. Jack, you must understand where its inspiration comes from—the Lyonnaise *bouchons* of France. These are not uptight restaurants. They're not lowbrow bars. They're a cultural tradition all their own, centered on a spirit of joyous indulgence. Bone marrow, truffles, pâte, foie gras, and meats swaddled in pastry: these are rich cornerstones of the cuisine, and it's not unheard of to find several married together in one dish. What you won't find are tweezers being employed, or nouveau-size portions, because in a *bouchon*, as at St. Jack, excess equals hospitality.

Chef-owner Aaron Barnett fully embraces that *bouchon* spirit, from the comfortable décor, to the luxe ingredients, to the over-sized plates. Steak frites always come topped with béarnaise sauce *and* from-scratch veal

demi-glace, but sometimes he puts this dish on the menu in a shareable size, topped with shank of roasted bone marrow and an optional slab of seared foie gras. But Barnett swings the other way, too, with dishes such as delicate albacore crudo or elegant seasonal salads of potato and crab with snap peas and buttermilk. Here the excess comes not from calories but from layers of flavor.

Two-year-old La Moule picks up where St. Jack leaves off, with a more pared-down and casual, bar-focused menu of moules frites, bistro burgers, and butter lettuce salad. But this time Barnett partnered with Tommy Klus, one of the city's best bartenders, making the craft cocktail list at La Moule just as big of a draw as the food.

Pictured: Roasted Côte de Porc with Curried Peach and Rose Petals

Roasted Côte de Porc with Curried Peach and Rose Petals *Serves 4*

Aaron Barnett's style of cooking at St. Jack can be summed up in one word: luxurious. Everything he makes at his French restaurant is a multilayered masterpiece of rich flavors and components, including this exquisite pork dish. It's made with peaches roasted in a sweet blend of brandy and brown sugar, then bathed in a buttery curry sauce spiked with the fruit's juices. In the spirit of the *bouchon,* the pork chops are cut big, for sharing, and the dish is served family-style.

Note: Vadouvan is a French curry powder made with dried shallots, onions, and garlic, along with fenugreek, curry leaves, cumin, and sweet spices like cinnamon, cardamom, and cloves. You can order it from online retailers.

PORK In a medium saucepan, combine the water, brown sugar, salt, garlic, and bay leaves. Squeeze the lemon and orange juice into the pan, then toss in the rinds. Bring to a simmer set over medium-high heat, stirring to dissolve the salt and sugar, then remove from heat and allow to cool completely. Combine the pork and brine in a large bowl or ziptop bag. Refrigerate for 24 to 36 hours. Remove from the refrigerator about 20 minutes before cooking.

PEACHES Preheat oven to 375°F. Combine the brown sugar, cumin seeds, cinnamon, cardamom, star anise, wine, and brandy in a baking dish (it should have the texture of very wet sand). Place the peaches, cut side down, on the mixture and roast for 8 to 12 minutes, until just tender. Remove the peaches with a slotted spoon, cut each peach into thirds, and set aside. Strain out the spices and reserve the juices. Keep the oven on.

PORK

2 cups water
1 cup packed brown sugar
¼ cup salt
4 cloves garlic, crushed
2 bay leaves
½ lemon
½ orange
2 (1 lb) double-cut, bone-in
    pork chops

PEACHES

1 ½ cups packed brown sugar
1 tsp cumin seeds
1 stick cinnamon, broken up
3 to 4 pods cardamom
2 star anise
1 cup white wine
¼ cup brandy
2 ripe peaches

ASSEMBLY

2 tsp vegetable oil
3 Tbsp unsalted butter (divided)
2 cloves garlic, one whole and
    one finely chopped
1 tsp finely chopped shallot
½ cup pork or chicken stock
1 Tbsp vadouvan or good curry
    powder (see Note)
1 red rose (not sprayed with
    pesticides), petals pulled off,
    torn in half or thinly sliced
1 tsp chopped fresh Italian parsley

ASSEMBLY Remove pork from the brine and pat dry. Heat the oil in a large sauté pan over medium-high heat. Add the pork and cook, undisturbed, for 6 minutes, until seared to golden brown. Flip over and sear for another 3 minutes.

Add 1 tablespoon of the butter and the whole garlic clove to the pan. Place in the oven and roast for 30 minutes, basting twice with the pan juices, until the internal temperature is 145°F. Allow to rest while you make the sauce.

Heat 1 tablespoon of the butter in another sauté pan over medium-high heat. Add the chopped garlic, shallots, peach juices, pork or chicken stock, and vadouvan. Allow to simmer for about 4 minutes, or until reduced by half. Add the pork and peaches and heat until warmed through.

Add the torn rose petals and chopped parsley. Add the remaining tablespoon of butter and swirl the pan to emulsify the butter into the sauce. Taste and adjust seasonings if desired. Arrange the peaches and sauce on the bottom of a large serving dish and arrange the pork on top.

INGREDIENTS

1 ½ oz Bowmore Small Batch scotch

½ oz Cynar

½ oz Punt e Mes vermouth

½ oz Combier Roi René Rouge cherry liqueur

Dash of Regans' orange bitters

Ice

1 wide strip fresh orange peel, 2 to 3 inches
    long, for garnish

Scotch Lodge

Serves 1

One of Tommy Klus's most popular cocktails, the Scotch Lodge is like an elevated Rob Roy. He's taken the pared-down classic and given it a bit more oomph with the addition of bittersweet Cynar and juicy Combier Roi René Rouge cherry liqueur.

METHOD Combine the scotch, Cynar, vermouth, cherry liqueur, and bitters in a mixing glass. Add ice and stir for 30 seconds, or until well chilled. Strain over a big ice cube into a double old fashioned glass. Hold the orange peel over the cocktail and lightly squeeze it along its midline to express the aromatic oils into the glass. Rub it over the glass rim, then drop it into the drink.

Multnomah Whiskey Library

ANH LUU & CHANTAL ANGOT
Tapalaya

UNTIL RESTAURATEUR Chantal Angot opened Tapalaya in 2008, no one in Portland thought to put a small-bites spin on Creole classics. And until chef Anh Luu took over the stoves, no one thought to put a Vietnamese spin on them either. But both concepts turned out to be brilliant moves, as the city can't get enough of this vibrantly hued, laid-back Mardi-Gras party in restaurant form.

At first it was a head-scratcher when word got out that Luu was stirring shrimp paste into her étouffée and sliding a pork belly bánh mì next to the fried oyster po'boys on the menu. What does Vietnamese food have to do with New Orleans? A lot, it turns out. For tens of thousands of Vietnamese war refugees in the 1970s, Louisiana was the promised land, where the Gulf Coast climate felt like home and where fellow Catholics welcomed them with

open arms. It wasn't long before the cuisines and cultures intertwined, and for people like Luu, the New Orleans–born daughter of war refugees, the kitchen was a place where fish sauce and filé powder lived in harmony.

With Angot's support and encouragement, Luu opened Portland's eyes to a side of Creole cuisine we had never seen before. And now we, too, crave a little lemongrass in our gumbo and five-spice on our blackened shrimp. Lucky for us, we have Tapalaya.

GRITS

4 cups whole milk

4 cups water

½ cup (1 stick) cold unsalted butter

2 cups stone-ground white grits
  (Bob's Red Mill)

1 Tbsp salt

½ cup heavy cream

SAUCE

1 Tbsp extra-virgin olive oil

6 cloves garlic, finely chopped

1 ¼ cups white wine

¾ cup chicken broth

1 ⅛ cups Crystal hot sauce (see Note)

1 Tbsp freshly squeezed lemon juice

2 Tbsp Creole seasoning (such as
  Seafood Magic or Cajun's Choice)

½ cup heavy cream

6 Tbsp (¾ stick) cold unsalted butter,
  cut into cubes

1 lb crawfish meat, rinsed

Crawfish Anh Luu

Serves 4 to 6

Chef Anh Luu didn't just put her own stamp on this New Orleans Jazz Fest favorite, she put her name on it too. It's just that personal. The dish of crawfish meat bathed in a creamy, spicy sauce is a riff on the famed Crawfish Monica created by Pete and Monica Hilzim of Kajun Kettle Foods in Baton Rouge. Luu worked at their Kajun Kettle stand throughout her college career, and her even richer adaptation, which also swaps out pasta for creamy grits, is an ode to the iconic dish. Frozen crawfish meat is usually available at local seafood markets. If it isn't available, simply substitute 1 pound of shrimp.

Note: Don't balk at using this much Crystal hot sauce, and don't use a substitute. The Cajun staple isn't as scorching hot as some other brands.

GRITS In a large saucepan, combine the milk, water, and butter over medium-high heat and cook until butter is melted. Once melted (and before the mixture comes to a boil), add the grits and whisk continuously for 5 minutes, until thickened. Reduce heat to low and cook, stirring occasionally, for

30 to 45 minutes, until the grits look glossy on top. Whisk in the salt and heavy cream until creamy. Keep covered on low heat until ready to serve.

SAUCE In a large skillet, heat the oil and garlic over medium-high heat until the garlic begins to sizzle. Add the white wine, chicken broth, hot sauce, lemon juice, and Creole seasoning. Bring mixture to a boil and simmer until reduced to about 1 cup. Add the heavy cream, bring back to a boil over high heat, and boil until the mixture thickens, the bubbles get bigger, and it looks darker around the edges. Reduce heat to low and whisk in the butter, one cube at a time. Stir until melted and incorporated. (Do not boil or the butter might separate. Moving the pan on and off the heat will help prevent your sauce from breaking.)

Add the crawfish and heat until warmed through. (If using shrimp, cook for 3 to 4 minutes, or until cooked through.) Remove from the heat and serve over grits.

INGREDIENTS

⅓ cup vegetable oil

2 lb bone-in, skin-on chicken thighs

1 lb Andouille sausage, sliced into
  ½-inch-thick slices

⅔ cup all-purpose flour

1 large onion, diced

3 stalks celery, diced

½ red bell pepper, diced

½ green bell pepper, diced

9 cloves garlic, finely chopped

2-inch piece fresh ginger, peeled
  and grated (about 3 Tbsp)

1 stalk lemongrass, finely chopped

2 tsp cayenne

1 Tbsp smoked paprika

2 Tbsp garlic powder

2 Tbsp Creole seasoning (such as
  Seafood Magic or Cajun's Choice)

2 bay leaves

3 qt chicken broth

2 Tbsp Sriracha

2 Tbsp Worcestershire sauce

3 Tbsp fish sauce (Tapalaya uses
  Three Crabs brand)

1 tsp freshly squeezed lemon juice

1 lb medium shrimp (41/50 count),
  peeled and deveined

1 lb fresh okra, sliced (about 2 cups)

Steamed rice or cornbread, for
  serving

Chicken, Shrimp, and Andouille Sausage Gumbo *Serves 8 to 10*

As chef Anh Luu says, "A good gumbo starts with a good roux." That's why she cooks hers good and long, adding onions so they'll caramelize right in the mix. Though her gumbo isn't quick to make, it freezes well, making leftovers the perfect dinner on a busy, rainy weeknight. Gumbo is traditionally served with rice or cornbread, but Luu says it's great with potato salad too.

METHOD   Heat the oil in a large, heavy-bottomed Dutch oven set over medium heat. Add the chicken, skin side down, and cook for 15 minutes, until golden brown. Turn and cook the other side until cooked through, about 15 minutes more. Transfer the chicken to a plate. In the same pot, cook the sausage over medium heat for 5 minutes, until browned. Transfer to the plate with the chicken. Refrigerate until ready to use.

Reduce heat to medium-low. Add the flour to the fat in the pot and stir to make a roux. Cook the roux, stirring occasionally, for about 1 hour, until it's caramel in color. Add the onions and continue to cook, stirring about every 15 minutes, until the roux turns dark brown, about 45 minutes more. Increase heat

to medium, add the celery, bell peppers, and garlic, and cook for 10 minutes until tender.

Stir in the ginger, lemongrass, cayenne, smoked paprika, garlic powder, Creole seasoning, and bay leaves. Add the chicken broth a little at a time, scraping up the browned bits and allowing the roux to absorb the liquid before adding more. Add Sriracha, Worcestershire sauce, fish sauce, and lemon juice. Taste and adjust seasonings if desired. Increase heat to medium-high and bring the gumbo to a boil to activate the roux, stirring frequently. Reduce the heat to medium and simmer for 15 minutes.

Meanwhile, remove the chicken from the bones and cut into chunks. Add the chicken, sausage, and shrimp to the gumbo and simmer for another 10 minutes, until shrimp are cooked through. Add the okra and simmer until tender and gumbo has thickened, about 5 more minutes.

Taste the gumbo and add more fish sauce, if desired. (It will enhance the seafood flavor in the shrimp and add saltiness.) Ladle the gumbo into bowls and serve alongside rice or cornbread.

JOHN GORHAM
Toro Bravo

IT ALL STARTED WITH THE BULL.
Chef-restaurateur John Gorham was by all means a heavy-hitting industry veteran by the time he opened his first solo project, Toro Bravo, in 2007. But it wasn't until he opened those bull-emblazoned doors that he earned a reputation for having a Midas touch. Born from Gorham's travels through Spain, Toro Bravo was an instant success, blending Spanish tradition with Northwest seasonality plus a healthy dose of Portland spirit.

In the 10 years since it opened, the city's hunger for Toro's seasonally inspired tapas has never ceased, and Gorham's drive has yet to wane. In fact, he's added an entire roster of restaurants all over town: the worldly yet comforting Tasty n Sons, the steakhouse-inspired Tasty n Alder, the snazzy PLAZA DEL TORO event space/gastronomic society, the Middle Eastern–inflected Mediterranean Exploration Company, its fast-casual spin-off Shalom Y'all, and the newest addition — Bless Your Heart Burgers, poised to give Shake Shack a run for its money. But at the beating heart of this growing empire is Toro Bravo, the perennially packed restaurant that started it all.

Pictured: Three Spanish Tapas with Aioli

MEJILLONES EN ESCABECHE
"MUSSELS FRITES"
Vegetable oil, for deep-frying
½ cup aioli (see here)
2 tsp ground piment d'Espelette
4.9 oz can Ramón Peña mussels in
   escabeche
2 Tbsp Caviaroli Espelette (see Note)
1 large russet potato, peeled, thinly
   sliced into matchsticks on a mandoline,
   and soaked in cold water overnight
Salt
Chives, finely chopped

Three Spanish Tapas with Aioli *Serves 2 to 6*

Anyone who's been to Spain knows that country has mastered the art of preserving its bounty of seafood into little tins of exquisite *conservas*. Chef John Gorham put together this trio of simple tapas to show just how amazing Spain's canned seafood delicacies can be. Each serves about two people, or make all three and have a cocktail party. Look for the seafood and spices at gourmet shops with a strong selection of imported Spanish goods, or through online retailers.

Note: Caviaroli is olive oil that has been encapsulated into little spheres to mimic the texture of caviar. A product that has been served at Spain's famed El Bulli restaurant, it comes in several flavors, including Espelette pepper. You can find it through online retailers.

MEJILLONES EN ESCABECHE "MUSSELS FRITES" In a large saucepan or deep fryer, heat at least 2 inches of oil to 375°F (this can take up to 20 minutes). Keep a plate lined with paper towels nearby.

Meanwhile, in a small bowl, combine the aioli and ground Espelette. Spoon the seasoned aioli onto one side of a large plate. Arrange the mussels on top of the aioli, then spoon over the Caviaroli.

Strain potatoes from the water and dry thoroughly. When oil is ready, add a handful of potatoes to the hot oil. Working in batches, fry until they're beginning to brown and crisp and they stop releasing steam, about 2 minutes. Transfer the potatoes to the plate lined with paper towels to drain. Season with salt and chives and repeat with the remaining potatoes. Place on the opposite side of the plate from the mussels.

SARDINES WITH PADRÓN PEPPERS

½ cup aioli (see here)

4.6 oz can Ramón Peña sardines in olive oil

1 Tbsp extra-virgin olive oil

2 cups (1 pint) Padrón peppers

Sea salt

Edible flowers, for garnish (optional)

SPANISH MACKEREL CONSERVA

½ cup aioli (see here)

4.9 oz can Ramón Peña Spanish mackerel in olive oil

Small handful of pea shoots or 1 bunch watercress, root ends trimmed

2 tsp freshly squeezed lemon juice

1 Tbsp extra-virgin olive oil

Salt and freshly ground black pepper

Edible flowers, for garnish (optional)

AIOLI

4 cloves garlic

1 tsp salt

¼ tsp lemon zest

1 Tbsp freshly squeezed lemon juice

4 egg yolks

1 ½ cups safflower oil

½ cup extra-virgin olive oil

SARDINES WITH PADRÓN PEPPERS

Spoon the aioli onto one side of a large plate. Arrange the sardines on top of the aioli. Heat the olive oil in a large skillet over high heat until almost smoking, then add the peppers. Sauté, tossing regularly, until the peppers are blistered and fragrant. Remove from heat, season with coarse sea salt, and stack them up nicely on the other side of the plate. Garnish the plate with edible flowers, if using.

SPANISH MACKEREL CONSERVA

Spoon the aioli onto one side of a large plate. Arrange the mackerel on top of the aioli.

In a bowl, toss the pea shoots with the lemon juice and olive oil. Season with salt and pepper to taste and place on the other side of the plate. Garnish with edible flowers, if using.

AIOLI Combine the garlic and salt in a mortar and use a pestle to smash into a paste. Add the lemon zest, juice, and egg yolks. Wrap a damp towel around the base of the mortar to prevent it from moving. While whisking briskly, add a few drops of the safflower oil at a time until it begins to thicken up. (Alternatively, you can use a food processor, or add the garlic paste to the bowl of a mixer fitted with the whisk attachment and proceed from there.) While whisking (or processing), slowly add the rest of the safflower oil in a very thin, steady stream. If the mixture begins to tighten and resembles overly thick mayonnaise, add a little water to loosen it up a bit.

Gradually add the olive oil in a steady stream while whisking gently (or processing). Taste and add more salt and lemon juice if necessary. Add a little water if it's too thick. (It will thicken considerably if refrigerated, but can be thinned to your liking at any point with a little water.)

Sopa de Ajo

Serves 8

Buying a whole chicken and cutting it up yourself not only is cheaper, but means you'll have pieces left over to make flavorful soups like this. Just store them in the freezer until you have enough. The stock forms a rich base perfect for floating rustic garlicky croutons and poached eggs. It also makes delicious use of leftover rotisserie chicken. A little pork, in the form of bacon, chorizo, or ham, adds incredible flavor, and the chicken feet (order from your butcher) give the soup silkiness thanks to their natural gelatin. Although this recipe serves a crowd, don't feel obligated to throw a party. Poach only as many eggs as you need and freeze the leftover stock for another day. Leftover croutons will keep all week in an airtight container. Throw them in green salads or use them as the base for panzanella.

STOCK Combine all the ingredients, except the salt, in a large stockpot. Cover with cold water by 2 to 3 inches and bring to a simmer over high heat. Reduce to medium heat and simmer for 6 to 8 hours, skimming the foam from the surface. (If you're in a hurry, increase the simmer slightly and simmer for about 4 hours.) Add water, if necessary, to keep the bones submerged.

Strain the liquid into a medium pot and discard the solids. Heat the stock over medium-high heat and simmer for about 30 minutes, until reduced by about 20 percent. Season with salt to taste.

STOCK

2 ½ lb chicken necks and backs

1 ½ lb roasted or rotisserie chicken
(meat and bones)

½ lb chicken feet

3 oz bacon, Spanish chorizo, and/or
serrano ham

4 to 5 bulbs garlic, top third sliced
off to expose the cloves

Salt

GARLIC-PIMENTÓN CROUTONS

6 Tbsp (¾ stick) unsalted butter

6 Tbsp extra-virgin olive oil

20 cloves garlic, roughly chopped

2 Tbsp smoked paprika (pimentón)

1 loaf rustic bread, crust removed
and torn into bite-size pieces
(about 10 cups)

POACHED EGGS

1 tsp distilled white vinegar

8 eggs

ASSEMBLY

Finely chopped chives,
for garnish

Hot sauce, for drizzling
(Toro Bravo uses house-
made fermented hot sauce)

GARLIC-PIMENTÓN CROUTONS Preheat oven to 325°F. Combine the butter and the olive oil in a small saucepan set over medium-low heat. When the butter has melted, add the garlic and simmer for 20 minutes until the garlic smells sweet and has lost its raw pungency.

Add the smoked paprika and remove the pan from the heat. Stir well and let the mixture sit for a few minutes to bloom the paprika and infuse the fat with its flavor. Strain the fat through a fine-mesh strainer into a bowl and add the torn bread. Toss well to coat. Season the croutons with salt and place in an even layer on two baking sheets. Bake for 20 to 30 minutes, stirring occasionally, until golden brown. (It is okay if the centers are a little chewy.)

POACHED EGGS Bring a large skillet of water to a steady simmer over medium-high heat and add the vinegar. Crack an egg into a ramekin or cup. Slowly tip the egg into the water, whites first. Repeat with the remaining eggs. When whites begin to set, use a rubber spatula to gently move them around to prevent them from sticking. Cook at a slow simmer for 3 to 4 minutes, until the whites are completely set and yolks are soft but no longer raw.

TO SERVE Set one egg into each bowl. Surround with five to seven croutons and ladle about 1 cup of broth over the top. Serve with chives and a drizzle of hot sauce.

LIZ DAVIS & KELLY MYERS

Xico

ON WARM SUMMER NIGHTS, when the front doors are wide open to the breeze and the patio lights are twinkling in the oasis out back, dining at Xico feels like a vacation. With its clean lines, white walls, and platters of Mexican food so vibrant, fragrant, and complex, you could easily pretend you're at an upscale restaurant in Mexico City. And on cold winter nights, when the rain just won't let up, the glowing restaurant beckons you in and transports you once again, warming you up from the inside with *queso fundido* topped with spicy chorizo, or juicy chicken drenched in rich mole, a stack of fragrant housemade tortillas on the side for sopping up all the sauce.

This is the magic of Xico, a place that never gets old and never ceases to please. A place that upholds the flavors and traditions of Mexican cuisine, from the mezcals to the moles, without feeling either overly earnest or theme-parky. Ever since owner Liz Davis and executive chef Kelly Myers opened Xico in 2012, well before Division Street's restaurant renaissance, they've managed to successfully blend the seasons and ingredients of the Northwest with the rigors of authentic Mexican cooking. It's seasonal, experimental, and playful, and exactly what the city craves all year long.

Pictured: Sopa de Lima with Shrimp and Habanero

Sopa de Lima with Shrimp and Habanero

Serves 4 to 6

If you make your fish stock in advance, this incredibly flavorful soup comes together in no time. The secret is in the *sofrito,* a flavorful mix of sautéed peppers, garlic, tomato, and spices. Studded with tender shrimp and garnished with diced avocado, crispy chips, and a couple teaspoons of habanero-spiked lime juice, it'll liven up the dinner table any time of year.

Notes: Call your fishmonger to reserve bones, heads, and tails from whitefish such as halibut, cod, snapper, and sole. Avoid bones from oily fish such as salmon, which are too strongly flavored. Be sure to rinse off any blood before using. You can also soak them in cold water mixed with 1 tablespoon salt for 1 hour to purge the blood. Rinse well. | Achiote seed is also called annatto. You can find packages of it in the spice section at Mexican markets.

FISH STOCK Remove the shells from the shrimp and set aside. Refrigerate the shrimp until ready to use.

Heat the oil in a stockpot set over medium-low heat. Sauté the onions, celery, carrots, and achiote seed for 10 to 15 minutes, until softened. Add the garlic and sauté for 3 minutes.

Add the shrimp shells and whitefish bones and heads, stir, and cook until the shells begin to turn pink. Add the wine, tomatoes, cilantro, and cold water. Bring to a simmer over high heat, reduce to medium-low, and cook, uncovered, for 30 to 40 minutes.

Strain the stock through a colander set over a large bowl, and discard the solids. Allow to cool, and skim off any fat that rises to the surface. You should have 6 or 7 cups. Top off with water if necessary. (Stock can be made several days ahead. Allow to cool, then refrigerate. Scrape off any fat that solidifies on the surface before using or freezing for longer storage.)

FISH STOCK

Makes 7 cups

1 ¾ lb medium shrimp (41/50 count),
   shells on

1 Tbsp vegetable oil

½ white onion, roughly chopped

½ stalk celery, roughly chopped

1 carrot, roughly chopped

½ tsp achiote seed (see Note)

2 cloves garlic, crushed

2 ½ lb whitefish bones and heads
   (see Note), rinsed

¼ cup white wine

2 whole fresh or canned Roma
   tomatoes

½ bunch fresh cilantro leaves

2 qt cold water

SOPA

1 Tbsp extra-virgin olive oil

½ white onion, finely chopped

1 green bell pepper, diced

2 cloves garlic, finely chopped

2 Roma tomatoes, peeled, seeded,
   and chopped

1 tsp salt

⅛ tsp freshly ground black pepper

⅛ tsp Mexican oregano

⅛ tsp ground cloves

⅛ tsp ground allspice

2 bay leaves

Zest of ½ lime

6 to 7 cups fish stock (see here)

CHILE CON LIMA

3 habanero peppers

½ cup freshly squeezed lime juice

Pinch of sea salt

ASSEMBLY

Fresh cilantro leaves, for garnish

1 avocado, diced

30 totopos or tortilla chips,
   to serve

SOPA Heat the oil in a saucepan over medium heat. Add the onions and bell peppers and sauté, stirring occasionally, for 5 minutes, until the onions are translucent. Add the garlic and sauté for another minute, until fragrant. Add the tomatoes, salt, pepper, oregano, cloves, allspice, and bay leaves and cook for about 8 minutes, until the tomatoes are softened. Add the lime zest and cook for another minute.

Stir in the stock and bring to a simmer over medium-high heat. Reduce to medium-low and simmer for 10 minutes. Cut the shrimp crosswise into thirds. Stir in the shrimp and cook for 3 minutes, or until the shrimp are cooked through.

CHILE CON LIMA Wearing protective gloves, slice the habanero peppers crosswise into very thin rings. Combine the peppers, lime juice, and salt in a small nonreactive bowl. Allow to marinate for 30 minutes. (The condiment is intended to be very hot. One way to enjoy it with less heat is to spoon just some of the lime juice into your soup, avoiding the chiles.)

ASSEMBLY Divide the sopa among bowls. Garnish with cilantro, diced avocado, and fried *totopos* or tortilla chips. Serve with chile con lima on the side, for drizzling.

Chicken with Mole Amarillo and Summer Vegetables *Serves 4*

Xico is known for refined takes on Mexican classics, and this beautiful dish is one of its best sellers. At the restaurant, they serve the vibrant Oaxacan mole with rotisserie chicken and delicate tortillas made from freshly ground masa, but it's just as delicious with a simple poached chicken and sautéed vegetables.

Notes: All lard is not created equal. The shelf-stable lard sold in tubs is devoid of flavor, so don't even bother. If you're not up to the task of rendering your own lard from pork fat, seek it out from quality meat markets and butcher counters. | You can find fresh masa at some Mexican markets, and in Portland it's available in several local grocery stores and co-ops from Three Sisters Nixtamal. If you can't find it, you can make your own with masa harina flour. Follow the directions on the package.

CHICKEN Bring chicken broth to a simmer in a large pot. Add the chicken, weight it down with a plate, and poach for 35 minutes, until cooked through. Transfer to a cutting board. Reserve the cooking liquid to use in the mole. When cool enough to handle, cut the chicken into 10 serving pieces — drumsticks, thighs, wings, and breasts cut into quarters. (The back can be reserved for making stock.)

MOLE AMARILLO In a cast-iron skillet set over medium-high heat, add the allspice, cloves, cumin, and oregano and toast for 15 seconds. Transfer to a blender.

In the same skillet, add the chiles and toast for 1 minute, or until fragrant. Fill a bowl with hot water and submerge the chiles. Soak for 30 minutes, until softened. Drain and place in the blender along with the spices.

Meanwhile, in the same skillet, toast the tomato, turning, until soft and blistered with black spots. Add to the blender. Repeat with the tomatillos. Dry-toast the garlic with the

CHICKEN

2 qt chicken broth

3 lb whole chicken

MOLE AMARILLO

3 whole allspice

3 whole cloves

Pinch of cumin seeds

½ tsp Mexican oregano

9 dried guajillo chiles, stems and
   seeds removed

1 Roma tomato

3 small tomatillos

4 cloves garlic

½ white onion, cut into six wedges

6 to 8 cups chicken cooking liquid
   (divided), plus more for desired
   consistency

1 Tbsp good-quality lard (see Note)

½ cup fresh masa (see Note)

2 whole black peppercorns

ASSEMBLY

2 tsp extra-virgin olive oil

1 clove garlic, finely chopped

1 sprig fresh thyme, chopped

2 cups quartered chanterelle
   mushrooms or other mild-
   flavored wild mushrooms

½ eggplant, diced (2 cups)

skin on until soft and squeezable. Set aside to cool. When cool enough to handle, peel and add to the blender.

Dry-toast the onion until caramel-colored and softened. Add to the blender along with 1 cup of the chicken cooking liquid. Blend the ingredients until smooth; this may take 2 to 5 minutes. If necessary, add up to ¼ cup more broth to help the mixture achieve a smooth purée.

Pass the mole through a fine-mesh strainer set over a bowl to remove the chile and vegetable skins. (Mole base can be made up to this point 4 days ahead and refrigerated.)

Heat the lard in a heavy-bottomed pot set over medium heat, until almost smoking. Add the mole and sauté, stirring continuously, for 8 to 15 minutes, until the mixture has thickened and darkened a bit. (Watch out for splattering.) Whisk in 5 cups of the chicken cooking liquid and bring to a simmer. Cook for 3 to 5 minutes. Adjust consistency with additional chicken broth if necessary. The texture should be similar to half-and-half cream.

In a bowl, stir together the masa and about 1 cup of the mole until smooth. Stir into the pot with the rest of the mole and cook until thickened to the texture of potato soup, about 5 minutes. (Mole can be made up to this point a day ahead and refrigerated. If it thickens too much, thin it out with a little chicken broth when reheating.)

ASSEMBLY Heat the olive oil in a large skillet set over medium-high heat. Add the garlic and thyme and sauté for 2 minutes. Add the chanterelles and eggplant and sauté for about 8 minutes, stirring occasionally, until softened. Add the chicken and allow to warm through.

To serve, divide the chicken among four large shallow bowls. Spoon the mole over the chicken, and top with chanterelles and eggplant.

Conversion Charts

VOLUME

Imperial	Metric
⅛ tsp	0.5 ml
¼ tsp	1 ml
½ tsp	2.5 ml
¾ tsp	4 ml
1 tsp	5 ml
½ Tbsp	8 ml
1 Tbsp	15 ml
1 ½ Tbsp	23 ml
2 Tbsp	30 ml
¼ cup	60 ml
⅓ cup	80 ml
½ cup	125 ml
⅔ cup	165 ml
¾ cup	185 ml
1 cup	250 ml
1 ¼ cups	310 ml
1 ⅓ cups	330 ml
1 ½ cups	375 ml
1 ⅔ cups	415 ml
1 ¾ cups	435 ml
2 cups	500 ml
2 ¼ cups	560 ml
2 ⅓ cups	580 ml
2 ½ cups	625 ml
2 ¾ cups	690 ml
3 cups	750 ml
4 cups/1 qt	1 L
5 cups	1.25 L
6 cups	1.5 L
7 cups	1.75 L
8 cups	2 L

WEIGHT

Imperial	Metric
½ oz	15 g
1 oz	30 g
2 oz	60 g
3 oz	85 g
4 oz (¼ lb)	115 g
5 oz	140 g
6 oz	170 g
7 oz	200 g
8 oz (½ lb)	225 g
9 oz	255 g
10 oz	285 g
11 oz	310 g
12 oz (¾ lb)	340 g
13 oz	370 g
14 oz	400 g
15 oz	425 g
16 oz (1 lb)	450 g
1 ¼ lb	570 g
1 ½ lb	670 g
2 lb	900 g
3 lb	1.4 kg
4 lb	1.8 kg
5 lb	2.3 kg
6 lb	2.7 kg

LIQUID MEASURES

Imperial	Metric
1 fl oz	30 ml
2 fl oz	60 ml
3 fl oz	90 ml
4 fl oz	120 ml

LINEAR

Imperial	Metric
⅛ inch	3 mm
¼ inch	6 mm
½ inch	12 mm
¾ inch	2 cm
1 inch	2.5 cm
1 ¼ inches	3 cm
1 ½ inches	3.5 cm
1 ¾ inches	4.5 cm
2 inches	5 cm
2 ½ inches	6.5 cm
3 inches	7.5 cm
4 inches	10 cm
5 inches	12.5 cm
6 inches	15 cm
7 inches	18 cm
10 inches	25 cm
12 inches	30 cm
13 inches	33 cm
16 inches	41 cm
18 inches	46 cm

BAKING PANS

Imperial	Metric
5- × 9-inch loaf pan	2 L loaf pan
9- × 13-inch cake pan	4 L cake pan
13- × 18-inch baking sheet	33- × 46-cm baking sheet

CANS & JARS

Imperial	Metric
6 oz	170 g
28 oz	796 ml

TEMPERATURE

Imperial	Metric
90°F	32°C
120°F	49°C
125°F	52°C
130°F	54°C
140°F	60°C
150°F	66°C
155°F	68°C
160°F	71°C
165°F	74°C
170°F	77°C
175°F	80°C
180°F	82°C
190°F	88°C
200°F	93°C
240°F	116°C
250°F	121°C
300°F	149°C
325°F	163°C
350°F	177°C
360°F	182°C
375°F	191°C

OVEN TEMPERATURE

Imperial	Metric
200°F	95°C
250°F	120°C
275°F	135°C
300°F	150°C
325°F	160°C
350°F	180°C
375°F	190°C
400°F	200°C
425°F	220°C
450°F	230°C

Acknowledgments

WRITING A BOOK is an enormous undertaking, but producing a book is even harder. It took a large team of smart, talented people to help me grow *Portland Cooks* from an idea into the beautiful and dependable book you hold in your hands.

Big thanks first to publisher Chris Labonté, who tapped me for this project and was my cheerleader along the way, and to food writer and *Toronto Cooks* author Amy Rosen, whose candid advice gave me the courage to say yes.

From start to finish, the team at Figure 1 Publishing was phenomenal to work with and always had my back. Managing editor Lara Smith kept the chaos at bay and the trains running on time. Executive VP Richard Nadeau buoyed me when my spirits flagged. Michelle Meade's smart editing saved me from myself many times. Eagle-eyed copy editor Lana Okerlund made the book so clean it sparkles. Jessica Sullivan and Natalie Olsen brought it all to life with beautiful art direction and design. And marketing manager Mark Redmayne worked hard to introduce *Portland Cooks* to the rest of the world.

I owe a huge debt of gratitude to the army of cooks who generously offered their time and expertise to test all the recipes in this book and ensure each would be a success: Jodie Chase, Leslie Cole, Juno DeMelo, Sandi Francioch, Jolene George, Marnie Hanel, Sasha Kaplan, Sarah Kline, Ivy Manning, Carol Nelson, Wendi Nordeck, Beth Perkins, Cory Raiton, Abbie Rankin, JoAnna Rodriguez, Keith Sheets, Jen Stevenson (who doubled as a trusted confidante and wise consultant), and Cheri Swoboda.

Of course, no matter how good the recipes are, we eat first with our eyes, and photographer Leela Cyd made *Portland Cooks* a book to devour. Along with stylist Anne Parker and assistant Celeste Noche, she created an incredibly beautiful and varied collection of photos that capture the spirit of each dish and the people behind them. Watching them work was awe-inspiring.

They say herding cats is no easy task, but writing a cookbook with 40 different chefs (who spend most of their waking hours behind a stove, not a computer) has got to be far more difficult. Much gratitude goes to PR pros Michelle Broussard, Erica Perez, and Heather Jones for smoothing that process considerably. There were indeed many ups and downs, frustrations, and long hours, but I couldn't have had a better (and more patient) support team than my husband, Mike, and daughters, Emma and Audrey.

But all of this would be moot without the people we celebrate in these pages. Not only do these chefs make Portland one of the best dining destinations in the world, they put their faith in this project, and in me, and I will always be grateful.

Index

DANIELLE CENTONI is a James Beard Award–winning food writer, recipe developer, and cookbook author. She is a former food editor of the *Oakland Tribune*, the *Oregonian*, *Imbibe Magazine*, *MIX Magazine*, and *Eater Portland*. Her work has been featured in regional and national publications, including *EatingWell*, *Better Homes and Gardens*, *Modern Farmer*, and *Seattle Magazine*, among others. She has also co-authored three cookbooks and contributed editorial work and recipes to many others. She regularly blogs about home cooking in the Pacific Northwest at Roux44.com.